Praise for The Infinity Wave

"Hope Fitzgerald's landmark book, *The Infinity Wave: Mastering the Art of Love, Compassion and Flow*, is a wonder. With her signature clarity, humor, and deep intelligence, Hope describes the miracle of the Infinity Wave as a necessary tool for our times, a tool that is available to anyone in its simplicity, elegance and power. As both the conduit and master technician, Hope offers all one needs to understand and use this miraculous tool. Anyone who chooses can immediately access the love, compassion and flow contained in the Infinity Wave, and see instantaneous blessings as a result. How fortunate for us that Hope has delivered the Wave to the world!"

~ Dr Janice Seward
Psychotherapist & Metaphysical Practitioner

"Hope introduced me to this energetic years ago, when she was called to bring it to humanity. I was beyond fortunate to be in her orbit, for *The Infinity Wave* is perhaps the most brilliant and powerful tool for healing, personal expansion, and putting love into the world. This simple and life enriching practice has comforted me, grounded me, enhanced my relationships and connected me more deeply to Mother Earth, and our Universe. I am beyond grateful to Hope for listening to the call, and sharing it with the world. This book is so needed. It is a gift. And so is Hope Fitzgerald."

~ Barbara Newman, author, *The Dreamcatcher Codes*
(2022 Nautilus Book Award)

"Hope Fitzgerald offers us all great inspiration in her book, *The Infinity Wave: Mastering the Art of Love, Compassion and Flow*. In her authentic story she tells the story of how the Infinity Wave came to her, how to use the Infinity Wave, and lessons of life she has gained from her experiences. Simple yet profound, the Infinity Wave can lighten our struggles in life and strengthen our courage to be true to who we are and who we have come here to be through service. I recommend this book to all who want to use a heart centered tool daily to add ease and intention in all that they do."

~ Marypat E., St. Louis

"I woke up this morning thinking about my endless appreciation of the Infinity Wave. On the world stage we have the outer picture of divisiveness and war, but my everyday experience of this has been hugely improved by the Infinity Wave. Thank goodness I have the tool of sending it silently to everyone. I can keep my heart open by giving and receiving love and compassion inherent within it. I feel blessed to share this growing circle of life, love and light on Planet Earth and beyond."

~ Karen Brehm

Hope Fitzgerald's offerings are so wonderful! From dowsing to coaching to workshops and meditation, she has so much to offer. She's been a personal lifeline to me through many rocky life transitions and a powerful grounding presence to our company's upward movement in consciousness in countless ways. Every Monday I look forward to connecting with Hope through her meditations and am amazing at the loving community she has created and supported around the world. To know she is here with us and available to reach out to for support is one of the best gifts and resources I have in these tumultuous times. Thank you so much, Hope!

~ Jen Solin

the
infinity
wave

MASTERING THE ART OF
LOVE, COMPASSION, AND FLOW

Hope Fitzgerald

Powerful You!
PUBLISHING
Sharing Wisdom ~ Shining Light

The Infinity Wave
Mastering the Art of Love, Compassion, and Flow

Copyright © 2023

Published by: Powerful You! Inc. USA
powerfulyoupublishing.com

Library of Congress Control Number: 2023922525

Hope Fitzgerald—First Edition

Interior Drawings Provided By Sayzie Carr

ISBN: 978-1-959348-20-7

First Edition December 2023

SELF-HELP/ Spiritual

dedication

Dedicated to Jim, Riley, and Lily,
Thank you for blessing my life
with your presence;
my love for you is infinite.

table of contents

acknowledgments

No one does this sort of thing alone. If I hadn't had the supportive embrace of many dear souls (both embodied and not) along the way, I wouldn't be here today. It is a long list…

I must start by acknowledging my intrepid mother, Ginny, who opened the window into other worlds for me at a young age—little did she know how far I would fly through that opening! She respected my nine-year-old's desire to be brought to all the houses of worship in our town in my search for a spiritual home. She introduced me to self-improvement, the healing arts, "natural" cooking, herbology, seances, and pendulum dowsing, to name just a few, and all at a time when such things were said in hushed voices. From her suburban home, she hosted weekend retreats with the most "wuwu" folks you can imagine. (Wuwu is a respectful Chinese word meaning the village healer/shaman.) Although you're not physically here, Mom, I know you're very busy on the other side and I'm aware that you look in on me from time to time. You're an amazing soul, and I was gifted to have you as my one and only mother.

I also bow to my dear husband, Jim, who understood that I have a mandate and has stood by me through it all, sometimes urging me to get the book finished, sometimes brainstorming an idea or design, sometimes sitting back and letting me stew, sometimes willing to let me go off by myself for a few weeks to get concentrated work done. He has loved and supported me throughout the long process, and for that, I will always be eternally grateful. I love you.

I wouldn't be here today without the wisdom and guidance of my many teachers over the years. To name just a few who I've experienced in person, thank you to the Findhorn Foundation (specifically the late Bruce Davidson), Dr. Bertrand Babinet, Jorge Luis Delgado, Dr. N.V. Tyree, Carolyn Myss, Lisa Rafel (who also was my occasional writing buddy), Zacciah Blackburn, Gregg Braden, Joe Dispenza, and Dr. Wayne Dyer.

Two teachers stand out as especially meaningful and helpful. One is Dr. Patrice Fields, who for many years I've trusted to explain the multiple realities I've experienced along the way. I could say more, but for brevity's sake, she has rescued me (and my family) many times when I waded too far into the deep end and has lovingly cradled me in opening to my new role as a spiritual guide. I followed Patrice to various power spots on the planet, each time learning tremendous amounts due to her ability to read nature and land energies. Patrice is a unique, gifted, compassionate coach/mentor without whom I literally could not have survived the hurdles, twists, and turns, and alternate universes that came my way. I bow to you in gratitude and love, my dear colleague and friend.

The other is Tom Kenyon, who does not know that he changed my life. It was his weekend sound workshops that allowed me to go on an initiatory journey that paved the way for the Infinity Wave to enter my consciousness. He is a consummate communicator of spiritual consciousness and I hope someday to tell him in person how grateful I am for all he's taught me. He is a very special being, who has given me the courage to follow my higher calling by watching him follow his higher calling. Thank you, teacher and wayshower.

There's one woman who saw something in me before I ever did and had the grace to tell me about it. Dr. Jan Seward has been my rock, my gal pal, my laughing buddy, my deep-sea diver, my travel companion, and my personal oracle. My appreciation, admiration, and love knows no bounds—thank you, dear friend, for all you've done to help my journey and for getting this little book to flower into reality. YOU'RE THE BEST.

A great source of inspiration and support for me over the last eight years has been composer, Gary Malkin. I want to especially acknowledge not only his great friendship but the uplifting impact his music has on all the channeled meditations I do. Due to my experiences with Gary's music, I believe it has had an unquantifiable ability to support the evolution of our souls like no other medium. Thank you for sharing your extraordinary gift with me and the world, Gary!

Then, there's the long list of beautiful beings who dove into the deep end with me in the first year of Infinity Wave workshops in 2011, many of whom were also part of a weekly meditation group we had for five years. I won't mention each one by name here, but know that you intrepid souls were the fertile soil in which the Infinity Wave could take root, and I will never forget you. Without you, I would have no story to tell. You came to a workshop without an inkling of what you were in for and willingly, bravely jumped in with both feet. Wow. That's trust. That's love. I love you back! Thank you.

A handful of dear, long-time friends allowed me to voice my fears and reluctance at various junctures of my journey, and subsequently agreed to receive drafts of this book that I gingerly proffered for their comments. These beloveds regularly checked in to see how I was progressing, always kindly urging me forward. After eight years, you'd think they would have given up, but, no, these loyal souls hung in there, and ultimately gave me great feedback. Thank you for your loyalty, kindness, and support—I treasure you.

One of those is Barbara Newman, who coached me in finding a publisher and all things pertaining to getting a book done, including gently urging me to finish. Thank you for generously paving the way.

There are others who provided writing havens when I couldn't get focused at home—you know who you are. Bless you for your kindness!

I must also mention writing coach, Jennifer Broudy, who took me seriously long ago, and over the years kept after me to write while helping me to shape the narrative at various points. Thanks for your gentle persistence and excellent guidance.

There are two talented artists represented in this book, one of whom became a consummate doodler of the Infinity Wave from the very start (Susan Solovay), and another who joined up later (Sayzie Carr). Your combined mastery in translating the ideas into form have helped to make the tale more accessible and inspiring. Thank you both for your passion, willingness, and meticulous abilities. Muah!

Over the years, I was assisted by a very clever, talented

woman named Heather Flemming, who was responsible for not only graphics, websites, and running meditations behind the scenes (to name just a few tasks), but also for brainstorming some excellent ideas about how to get the Wave out there even more effectively. Having a person who can stay in their left brain was essential to do the kind of right-brained work required of me; put another way, when I was out of my literal mind, Heather stayed firmly rooted and anchored me beautifully. Thank you, Heather!

Hats off to my longtime friend, Patrick Durkin, without whom I could not have functioned in the early days of the Infinity Wave business. Once he grasped the Wave, he dedicated his time and expertise to helping me get the business off the ground. As you will discover, I had no interest in such things, but when given a task to share this energetic with the world, it required certain foundations in order to communicate it properly. Patrick guided me through that process and has stayed nearby ever since, always eager to generously offer advice and assistance. Deepest gratitude, dear Patrick!

This leads me to the woman who "got it" within a few minutes of explanation and opted to launch the Infinity Wave into the world: Jennifer McLean. There I was at a crowded holiday party in LA when the seas parted and Jennifer walked through the door. Strangely, everyone abruptly left the room, leaving us able to have a high-level, private chat for about twenty minutes, which ended with her giving me her card and saying she wanted to work with me. The rest of the story will unfold in the book, but I will always be eternally grateful to Jennifer for her clairvoyance and willingness to be the first to formally introduce the Infinity Wave, not to mention forcing me to buck up and do the job I apparently came here to do. Love you, Jenn!

Following that initial exposure from Jennifer, I wish to thank the many other show hosts who invited me onto their platforms. Each conversation was fruitful and enlightening—I appreciated how you leaned in to understand what this new thing called the Infinity Wave was.

I also wish to thank those who were once close to me but have opted to divest from our relationship over the course of time. Even though it was painful to lose you, I grew immeasurably as a result of your presence in my life, and for that, I bow in gratitude, sending you Waves of compassion and love.

Lastly, the support of my meditation tribe has buoyed me immeasurably over the years in accomplishing my goal to finish this book. Those in my online group were the first readers of a very rough draft and their positive feedback gave me the extra energy I needed to fully finish and launch this. I look forward to seeing your beautiful faces each week— thank you, dear souls!

introduction

It has taken many more years to finish this guidebook than it should have. I will explain the reasons later; for now let me just say how thrilled I am to finally be able to hand this over to you! I wrote a big chunk of it in 2020, while we were deep in the pandemic. Remembering those days when anxieties ran rampant as layers of social uncertainties piled up, often in conflicting ways, writing was a way to calm my mind and focus on what really mattered. I watched as warring factions intensified in the form of political parties, COVID strategies, and environmental tragedies, fueled by a media that relentlessly spread disaster scenarios. Fears and confusions were compounded by a heightened moment of reckoning with one of our oldest national wounds: racism. Through it all, truth was nearly impossible to ascertain. If there ever was a time for feeling unstable, both personally and societally, that was it.

Yet there was also a wealth of opportunity for spiritual growth during that time as we had to stare squarely at our greatest unspoken fear: our mortality. In our pre-quarantine lives, society as a whole danced and jigged as if there was no end to the crazy race we were engaged in. But with the world-wide lockdown, we were forced to take pause and consider who we were and why we were living the way we did. Stepping back for a wider view, what else might we have seen occurring then—and even now?

Perhaps we might observe that life was—and is—radically

shifting, likely never to return to what we knew, and we may come to understand that it is a long-overdue, necessary correction to humanity's course. Perhaps, as I believe, we are even now each being called to change *through* these chrysalis-like circumstances, hopefully to emerge into a new paradigm that vibrates on a higher level.

But how do we take this evolutionary step that is being asked of us?

One thing I do know: if this is indeed a pivotal moment for our world, we cannot adapt if we are rigid with fear.

For decades, I was on the lookout for a crucible that would shake the world into awareness. Then, in a sudden series of visions in late 2010, I was told that as a planet we would be facing a giant "push of evolution" in coming years, and that resistance to this push would only make things more difficult. Instead, I was advised that if I learned to "flow" with these crucial changes, things would go easier for me.

Miraculously, at the same time, I was given a great gift to help with this, a gift I was meant to share with the world: the Infinity Wave. I was told that this watery "figure eight" is a 10th Dimensional energetic containing a highly purified form of Love and Compassion in its flow. As a geometric shape, the eight naturally imbues Unity consciousness and balance (As Above, So Below).

In the beginning, it was hard for my human brain to accept that merely imagining a geometric shape could do anything, let alone impact reality. But as I played with it and shared it with others, I was amazed to find that it consistently raised frequencies and stimulated expansion. The Wave seemed to connect us directly with Source (please substitute the word you feel most comfortable with: God/Creator/All That Is/ Universe/Spirit, etc.) even while being firmly grounded in 3D reality—a state I call "multi-dimensional being." Indeed, over the course of my first year of observing and using the Infinity Wave, I became convinced that it was a powerful reality-shifter.

I now know that it is precisely THIS time for which the Infinity Wave was intended; I have seen it help people beautifully cope with the uncertainties and fears we are all facing. It has supported us in maintaining our equilibrium, while also rising to challenges with more grace and ease. Yes, the Earth is going through a grand transformation (and is evolving as well), but that does not mean we have to be prisoners in the process. The Infinity Wave allows room for play, joy, and freedom, regardless of external circumstances.

I believe we have all chosen to come into form at this exact moment to experience "Earth school" for our souls' education and expansion. Having opted to enter into this rather dense, polarized 3-Dimensional reality consisting of time, space, and gravity, we expected to have abundant opportunities to grow through major life lessons, even though we knew some might not feel survivable in the moment. But we were willing to take on the challenges because, more than anything else, we desired for our souls to evolve in significant ways.

Evolution implies moving from one state into a more complex, refined state, and necessitates leaving certain things behind to make way for what is new. However, in releasing what no longer serves, we sometimes experience resistance because humans do not like the uncertainty of change and would rather hang onto what is known. That is an understandable response because our past experience as humans has taught us that change required a great deal of time and pain. However, the process of evolution that we are now caught up in is happening extremely quickly and we simply do not have time to ponder and plod our way through. The pressure is building for us to evolve.

One thing I've learned from the Infinity Wave is that *change does not necessarily mean struggle*, nor do we have to approach it with dread. When we employ it, the Wave provides us with the swift, quickening energy needed to make leaps into the unknown, proving that profound change *can* happen quickly, smoothly, and even miraculously, as I have witnessed multiple times. Its watery flow is extremely useful in calming our systems enough to navigate losses and receive new information with tranquility, bringing tremendous freedom and the realization that we can create much more vastly than we ever imagined.

Best of all, when we let go of what is no longer useful and welcome that which is going to elevate us, we get closer to the highest expression of ourselves and what we came here to do.

Spiritual evolution is a choice, and sometimes a messy one; as spiritual teacher Craig Hamilton once said, "Everyone wants to be enlightened, but no one wants to change." It is not always easy to take it on, but if you fervently desire to fulfill the role you came here to play, then the chances are that you will want to evolve beyond where you are right now.

The "highest expression of yourself" may be unclear at this time, and you may be wondering how you will know what it is. Perhaps you are simply having a deep yearning that your life be an authentic reflection of who you are as a spiritual being.

As you work your way through the evolutionary Infinity Wave practices outlined in this guidebook, some of these questions may be answered when you develop better communication within your own being and become more in tune with your sense of purpose.

My understanding is that the Wave is a kind of scalar (Source) energy dwelling in the quantum (also called the Resonant Field), and as such, is instantaneously available, malleable, and programmable. Just as our ideas move faster than light, the Wave responds immediately to our thoughts and needs—physically, mentally, emotionally, and spiritually. Imagine being able to quickly shift from angst to calm, deliver highly purified love and compassion to your field, and lovingly and instantaneously connect to your Higher Self and others, all without speaking a single word.

If this all sounds too simple and easy to be true, I completely understand. I had the exact same reaction when I first encountered the visions and their information. However, isn't it true that sometimes the simplest things are the most impactful?

Light-workers who have been early adopters of the Infinity Wave tell me that nothing else works as swiftly to bring coherence to their healings and group work, whether in person or online, and this is my experience as well. Used more deeply, this humble method can also deliver a profound development of consciousness, providing a pathway to accelerated spiritual evolution. I know it is bold to say, but Wave Energy could be the next iteration of spirituality itself.

I am not the only one calling for an entirely new approach to spirituality, one without dualistic factions and dogma. The Infinity Wave is uncomplicated, accessible, and non-denominational—it enhances any religion, philosophy, and spiritual practice. As a symbol, it is incorruptible. No words need be spoken to employ it—all that is required is an imagination and an invitation to the Wave. I can foresee a harmonious future in which everyone enjoys bathing in Wave Energy all day long! For now, I hope you will just start to play with the Wave as you would any new concept, and watch your life begin to shift—it does not have to be believed in to work.

Evolving a species into a higher frequency requires multiple catalysts, which is where you come in. Each of us can use the Wave as a catalyst, serving as positive, balanced anchors amidst the chaos. I realize that it might seem that the efforts of one small person could not make a difference, but in the quantum and in Unity consciousness, everything we do affects everyone and everything, as demonstrated in the first Infinity Wave transmission I received:

"You cannot imagine the thrill it is to have you tune in with us, to know we are seen and heard. It brings us tremendous joy and we thank you for your availability and efforts on our behalf. Each person counts, each person who is drawn to be here will be making a huge

contribution to the others. Even if you do not believe you have a meaningful role to play, nothing could be further from the truth. Each one of you will be assisting the birth of the other. This work will require courage and it will demonstrate the efficacy of non-dual change (explained later). **The importance of each individual cannot be stressed enough: you are the lights! You will be called upon to use that light.** *The opportunity to receive direct information will be constant. Being a willing vessel is key. Your preparation is important; know that all of it will be for the higher good. Pay attention to your dreams and take time each day in silence to listen. Thank you."*

As you evolve and expand into an even brighter light, you are in turn affecting everyone and everything in this evolution process. It matters very much that you step forward onto your path as a channel to birth yourself, the Earth, and humanity into new and better possibilities. This may feel like a heavy responsibility, but it is also a happy, light-filled one because as we evolve, life becomes more rich and joyful, and we emanate that bliss out to all who surround us, even those at a distance.

Now, as we pull out of the pandemic into a world increasingly beset with uncertainty, the Infinity Wave can help smooth out confusion, fear, frustration, anger, and heartache, bringing us into a sustained state of inner harmony with each other and our world.

I offer this guidebook as an invitation for you to begin to play with this extraordinary energetic in hopes that it will become a great, trustworthy friend, in good times and bad. It is time to spread another kind of contagion: an energetic technology that might very well be the emblem of our age, now and going forward. We all need it.

~ Hope Fitzgerald

ONE
the infinity wave arrives

When the Infinity Wave suddenly appeared to me in a series of three visions in early November 2010, I seriously thought I might be losing my mind. I was at a particularly vulnerable moment in my life, having sustained numerous traumatizing events that year (in retrospect, it makes some sense that the Wave would find its way in through a weakened chink in my consciousness.) Even though I had been an ardent spiritual seeker for decades and was extremely open-minded to unusual activities of the Spirit, I was unprepared to *personally* experience visions until they literally stopped me in my tracks.

To preface the Wave's arrival, I have to go back a bit…

Because of the personal challenges of that year, I had embarked on a two-week healing journey with renowned sound healer, Tom Kenyon. I had no idea what to expect; all I can tell you is that I went into it with the single-minded intent on cleaning my "inner bowl" because I sensed I would develop an illness if I didn't release the detrimental emotions that had accumulated, not only that year, but throughout my entire life. I was on a mission to acquire a fresh slate.

1

Thankfully, by the last practice on the final day, I had not only removed tons of unnecessary and burdensome inherited beliefs, stories, and identities, but, more importantly, I had grasped the lessons within them. During Tom's last practice, I was so moved by my new level of understanding that, in my mind's eye, I went prostrate on the floor in loving gratitude and surrender to Source as these words sprang from my soul: "I am a willing vessel—do with me what You will."

I flew home a brand-new person and had three days of blissful emptiness…until I walked through my living room and abruptly "saw" a giant, one-hundred-foot-high wall of sparkling turquoise water, cresting gracefully as it slowly moved towards me. One could call it a tsunami, but it did not appear to be threatening in the least. If anything, it was beautifully mesmerizing to behold.

As it hovered above me, I became aware that there was a message associated with this vision:

"This Wave represents an energetic push that will be washing over the planet throughout 2011 until becoming anchored into the Earth at the end of the year. If one learns to swim with it or surf it instead of resisting, it will provide an opportunity for accelerated, smooth evolution. If not, it will be much more difficult."

Next, I saw a side view or cross-section of the curling wave resembling the letter "C"—think of a surfer skimming through a wave tunnel and you will get the idea. The accompanying message was:

"As the ocean water pulls away from the shore and

deepens down into the seabed to create a wave, so should you leave your knowledge (all that "book learning") on the shore and reach down into the ancient wisdom of the Earth for understanding. Look to the indigenous ones, the original wisdom keepers, for real knowledge."

As I continued to gaze at this C-shaped wave, I saw that the water did not fall directly back into the ocean as it normally would, but instead curled around to create a standing "figure eight" made of flowing ocean water, as pictured on the cover.

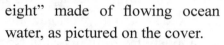

I was transfixed and wondered what the explanation of this striking image could be, but no further message appeared, even as it persisted in floating about eighteen inches in front of my forehead for the next few days. Finally, curiosity got the better of me and I consulted higher intelligence through dowsing to attempt to determine what this watery geometry was since it clearly was not going away.

A dowser for decades, I had developed a manner of inquiry that enabled me to ask questions beyond the usual "yes" and "no" variety. My dowsing rods were able to provide clear answers through nuanced responses, offering me words and visuals that steered me in certain directions. I guess you could say that the dowsing rods and my intuition worked together to discover what was important to understand.

In this way, I was told that the watery eight had a name, the Infinity Wave, and that it was a 10th-dimensional evolutionary tool for upcoming times of great change. Additionally, I learned that it was imperative for me to create a series of weekend workshops (one per month) from January through September 2011, during which this new energetic would be taught. The strong message was that this was something to be shared around the world, though I had no notion of how to accomplish this from my rural New England home.

I can't say I was thrilled with these directives and tried to reject them. Although I had been a leader all my life, the last thing I wanted to do was present myself as a spiritual guide. Even after five decades of study, I considered myself very much a student—I did not have a clue what I would teach or whether I was qualified to teach at all! There was virtually no information about the Wave to go on, certainly not enough to satisfy my usual need to be a well-prepared instructor. Suffice it to say, I was extremely uncomfortable with the whole idea.

The intense resistance that welled up in me revealed an underlying issue: even though I had read about and believed wholeheartedly in the miraculous, it was very hard to accept that something miraculous was actually happening *to me*. How could I be sure these were *real* communications "from beyond" and not mere imaginings?

Source had a way of making denial impossible—I literally felt a foot in my back pushing me forward into the unknown as I was reminded about my pledge as a "willing vessel." (Be careful what you say!) In my own personal earthquake, the familiar walls of my world started bending and re-shaping as my perceptions became stretched beyond recognition. In this new topsy-turvy existence, I felt as if I had a foot in two worlds and was not sure if there was such a thing as *'terra firma'* in either of them. Such is the tumble into other dimensions—it can be very disorienting and destabilizing.

My first lesson with this new information was to understand that there was no going backward, *and* the only way forward was to be in absolute trust that if I leapt, something would be there to catch me. Talk about testing my spiritual beliefs! Shakily, dutifully, and blindly, I finally leapt into the unknown by scheduling the first Infinity Wave weekend.

I must mention here that I was not entirely alone in this process, thank goodness. My dear friend and colleague, Dr. Jan Seward, was present for all of it, transcribing practices, interpreting divinations, assuring me that I wasn't losing my mind, co-leading the initial workshops and being a general grounding rod for all that was happening. I could not have done any of this without her and will always be indebted—even when I doubted, she didn't seem to, bless her.

My next job was to promote the workshop even though I had no idea of what the content would be or if anyone would be interested. Thankfully, in anticipation of that, another new phenomenon emerged: once a week I would sit down with Jan to dowse, but instead would enter into a semi-trance state while strange voices emanated from me, uttering words that were not my own. Jan would transcribe and provide feedback, as well as much-needed stability.

During these transmissions, I noticed that at times my doubting, human mind wanted to intercept and rearrange the wording, but something kept holding me out of the way so the language would be expressed purely. I had never considered myself a channeler, but now I slowly began to accept this as part of a new identity; these transmissions (or "downloads") ultimately became the foundational Infinity Wave meditations, known as The Original Practices. These weekly communications continued throughout the initial three months of weekend workshops…and beyond.

Since these channeled practices often referred to humanity's evolution, it occurred to me to add the word "conscious" in front of it. Though I couldn't see the full landscape at the time, I sensed we were heading into a paradigm in which each person would be carefully curating their own spiritual progression with newfound mindfulness. Wondering if I was the only one with this idea, I searched the Internet for "conscious evolution" and found only one entry, from visionary Barbara Marx Hubbard, though her interpretation of the term was entirely different from what I was gleaning. It seems odd now that we were ever without this concept, given the ubiquitousness of it today.

The same was true with the infinity symbol itself, of which I found no sign during my research in 2011. Then, in January 2012, infinity signs suddenly started showing up in popular culture, and grew in presence until today that symbol is virtually everywhere in jewelry, packaging, and logos— such is the way of collective consciousness! As a species, we have been tapping into something important with that symbol, though most people do not mentally understand why. I mention this because to attempt to communicate something new in spirituality has not only been a lonely journey, but at times also felt too grandiose, with my inner critic questioning, "Who do you think you are anyway?" Yet, regardless of my insecurities and turmoil, guidance kept pushing me forward.

Thinking about how to start the first weekend workshop, I found myself directed by my guide team to reach back thirty-five years to my classes at the Findhorn Foundation in Scotland. There, I had learned about evolution through the lens of Pierre Teilhard de Chardin—the early twentieth-century French "Renaissance man," Jesuit Priest, scientist, paleontologist, theologian, philosopher, and teacher. Today's scientific community may disagree with some of his theories; however, others still hold water.

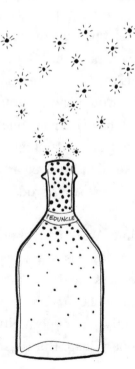

One of Teilhard's concepts that captivated me was the "peduncle," a biological term he used to demonstrate how all evolution was a spiraling, alchemical process of transitioning from one state into a more complex state. To imagine it, picture the peduncle where the wide part of the bottle begins to taper until it joins the neck.

7

Teilhard knew that all matter is in constant motion, so (according to my Findhorn instruction) he described how in the wider bottom of the bottle there are millions of atoms spiraling upwards, each one containing a "Godspark." As the atoms congregate evermore tightly on their approach to the narrowing neck, they collide with one another, causing friction. This friction and the rising momentum of the spiral pushes the atoms into the tight space of the bottleneck (the peduncle), where an alchemical process occurs: the atom transforms into a slightly larger, more complex entity—a molecule. Naturally, the "Godspark"—the innate aspect of Source in all living things—would also grow in size and energy.

In order for evolution to occur this birth canal process is then repeated over and over from the tiniest particle on up to *homo sapiens* and to where I believe we are now, the "Super-Human." This progression corresponds with our spiritual evolution as well—I believe most of us would say that our most challenging experiences (peduncles) have been the ones that have forced an expansive shift in our understanding of ourselves and of life itself. All I knew was that I was clearly being squeezed into my own "peduncle" and being prodded to dramatically transform.

As I prepared myself for the first Infinity Wave workshop, I hoped that if I integrated the Findhorn lessons, the latest scientific investigations into consciousness, and the new Infinity Wave channelings, I would produce a cohesive, compelling story—and, more importantly, an opportunity for the participants to make an evolutionary leap. But I also questioned whether this would inspire anyone or even make sense. It felt like my evolutionary surfboard was dizzyingly perched on the crest of that magnificent wave—I was about to take off down into the barrel of it, perhaps only to land flat on my face.

I remember my body shaking with fear as I entered the workshop space. I tentatively played a crystal bowl while delivering those initial guided meditations to the intrepid group members, to whom I will always be grateful for taking the leap with me. My loving guide team of non-physical beings were constant companions that weekend, giving me the courage to risk sharing their perspectives. Imagine my amazement when participants reported having powerful experiences from the very first practice! And, as the workshop continued, it became almost routine for there to be shared elements amongst them during the meditative journeys. We appeared to be occupying a new energetic bubble that we could all tangibly feel.

Even so, part of me was watching objectively like a scientist to see if this grand experiment would actually succeed. I withheld my complete commitment to the Infinity Wave work until I was certain that what I was witnessing would have lasting effects. Throughout that first year, participants (myself included) were indeed rewarded with speedy evolution as we all experienced smooth and significant transformations in our lives—peduncles were no longer so difficult when Wave energy was applied. As people's lives improved, their joy quotients went way up and even their faces were altered. We would stand back and rub our eyes at the speed of our progress—could this really be happening? Miracles became commonplace, and we realized that "we weren't in Kansas anymore," thanks to the use of the Wave as a tool for shifting realities.

My hesitance melted away as I became convinced that the Wave was precisely the evolutionary tool that it claimed to be in this transmission:

"I am the Infinity Wave and I wish to speak through you. I am the ebb and flow of Life itself. I exist in the realms beyond space and time, and yet contain space and time. I am ever mutable; I am ever in motion. My essence is indescribable. It is rather a sensation of movement felt and seen in reflection, experienced in reaction. This is why the metaphor of a wave is the closest approximation to what I am. Now, if you can, imagine that this ever-changing, ever-enlivening energetic of a wave contains what humans call emotions but on a much more distilled level. Picture the clarity of crystal and imbue that crystal with the thought of love—pure crystalline love—and now immerse that in the wave action and you begin to understand the incredible power and beauty of this energy. It is available for all— it already exists. It is simply now the job of each and every human being to open the mind to this reality that has always existed. It is the fundamental ingredient of Life. It is the well from which all Life springs.

Becoming one with the Wave does not mean there will be no pain—it means that you will move through your pain. It means there is a landing point, and a tumbling back into the Wave. You are always moving, going deeper into this infinite connection, not knowing how you will emerge but sure you will emerge, only to be tossed in again. Each time you venture forth to ride a wave you are a little wiser, a little better equipped to stay on your surfboard longer.

Share this journey. It is but the beginning of a whole new wave of existence for humanity and we are grateful for your willingness to tell the story... Doubt not. Doubt not. You are not alone."

Throughout those early workshops, we came to not just mentally understand, but *fully experience* that we humans are integral to the expansion of consciousness—that the Earth and the divine etheric realms express *through* us, not *to* us. We found that the Infinity Wave offered us a new orientation to personal growth—in a sense, we were a kind of beta test to try on this direct, dogma-free, hand-in-hand connection with Source.

The result for me was that I evolved into the knowing that this was to be my path for the rest of my life; my mandate (and honor) was to introduce the Infinity Wave to humanity. Confirmation of this came later that year when I happened to meet Jennifer McLean, who (I was to learn) at the time had the largest online international summit exploring consciousness. In our brief but impactful conversation she said, "You do know you've got one of the keys to the New Age, don't you?" I told her no, though if I'm being honest, I suspected it but was still nervous about accepting that level of responsibility.

Jennifer then told me she wanted to work with me. At the time, I had no idea who she was or what she did, so months later, when I finally visited her website, I was 'gobsmacked' to realize that my guides weren't kidding—the Infinity Wave was going to be released to Jennifer's 250,000 followers! There is no way I could have engineered such a thing by myself… I didn't even have a website. She was the one who provided a beautiful sound studio, a lovely, talented sound engineer, and a plethora of crystal bowls for me to play while I recorded the Infinity Wave practices. I had never felt so seen and supported. Many shows like hers ensued, but Jennifer started the ball rolling and pushed me to step up my game.

This entire process demanded a great acceleration of my own spiritual evolution, involving both internal and external shifts, and a complete dedication to living a spiritual life as a conduit to whatever wisdom wanted to pour through me, in service to whoever was interested. It continues to this day, thankfully—spiritual evolution was, and is, afoot!

TWO
spiritual concepts

In order to explain the Infinity Wave, I want to briefly share some spiritual concepts as I understand them, having been directly taught by wisdom keepers, my guide team, and through personal experience. They are by no means full explanations, but thimblefuls of ideas so that when I ultimately describe the Wave practices, we are using a common language.

Over decades of spiritual study and practice, I have looked for the similar themes between religions, philosophies, science, physics, and information from the etheric realms. I am not a scientist but have included those perspectives to arrive at many of my beliefs. Truly, there is so much we still don't know that nearly all of what follows is hypothesis. Ultimately, I have arrived at my own theories of "reality" and spirituality, but I hasten to add that my ideas are still developing; what I write here, in the *briefest* of summaries, is where I am so far.

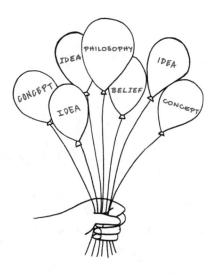

I do not ask you to completely agree with me—I am simply sharing my truths and if they are helpful for you in any way, they will have served their purpose. If any of these ideas meet some resistance within you, please simply place them in a "belief box" to be reviewed later. Humans have a proclivity for reaching a conclusion and then concretizing it in a box with a label—now that's solved! I submit that the mystery cannot, and should not, be handled this way. I often suggest that ideas be held like a bunch of helium balloons—you can keep thoughts in hand for consideration until such time that you choose to pull one into your consciousness to stay. For now, just allow the ideas to float harmlessly overhead.

A Brief Overview of Spiritual Evolution

With the hectic pace of modern life, it is often easy to forget that spiritual evolution is what we came to do here at the School of Earth. Buddhist monk and physicist, Marcus

Schmieke, said words to this effect: "When I realized that I came into this world with a soul and it's the only thing I will take out, I figured I'd better polish it well!" That "polishing" is specifically why I believe we chose to incarnate, and why life can sometimes feel quite daunting—it *has* to be in order for us to learn. After all, we do not grow without challenges— or should I say peduncles?

So, what does it mean to spiritually evolve?

My definition is that it is the transition from one spiritual awareness to another—an awakening, as if born anew, to a fresh view of "reality," which automatically and dramatically changes our relationship to it. Whether forced through circumstance or self-directed, evolution can happen in a sudden flash of insight and/or it can take focus and hard work—usually both. Think of those who have had near-death experiences (NDE), who often return from their visits to another existence with a sudden clarity about their lives and their purpose along with a renewed zest for life. Others take the life-long evolutionary path, fervently dedicating themselves to enriching their awareness and connection to Source throughout their struggles and joys. Some remain blissfully unaware of this process, but it affects them, nevertheless. There is no end to the journey—we carry our evolution with us into the next realms and beyond, ad infinitum.

Spiritual evolution is not a mental process, but a full-bodied awareness that is unique for each person and can happen multiple times in a life. Much like the well-worn metaphor of peeling the onion, each breakthrough revelation comes as we are ready to handle it and typically brings a full range of emotions, from ecstasy to devastating pain, while shattering previous convictions. We are forced to confront deep-seated beliefs, often hidden from our conscious minds, for their veracity and relevancy, and release those that no longer fit with our new perceptions. I think of these "shatterings" as "enlightenments" because for most of us, each onion layer brings us inextricably closer to the Truth of who we are and what we are meant to do here. With each shift in perspective, a new evolutionary trajectory is set in motion, with no retreating to earlier held beliefs—the toothpaste cannot go back in the tube.

I believe that spiritual evolution happens not in a straight, arcing, or circular line, but in a spiral. Gregg Braden writes in *Fractal Time* that time, as we think of it, also moves in a spiral.

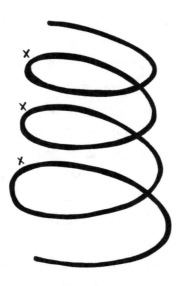

To paraphrase his concept, think back to a challenging event in your life as "Point X" on the first loop. Years later, as you round the bend to the same area on the next loop, you might experience an echo of what had occurred at the original spot but this time at a higher octave. As we ascend the rising spiral, we continue to have related versions of experiences at similar places on the spiral until we have adequately learned the lesson. Although the circumstances and players might be different, the themes are the same—we know we have achieved the growth from that situation when the issue no longer returns.

What is the ultimate purpose of all this spiritual education?

To return to our home, to Source, as pure beings of love and light. Many masters have taught us through their own journeys that we are here to remember who we are: not isolated individuals inhabiting an earthly form, but essential souls who are part of the whole of Creation, with all the wisdom, mystery, and love that that realm has to offer if we would only receive it. When Buddha sat under the Bodhi Tree, he became aware that he already existed within the heart of the Divine partly because he had completely surrendered himself to It. His long quest for enlightenment ceased when he stopped reaching for it and instead allowed Source into his heart. He evolved into being one with Creation, and so can we, if we surrender and accept this oneness, this home, as truly being available to us.

Going Direct

Ponder this...we all have inherited inclinations and

beliefs, and their resulting behaviors, from our lineage: our parents, their parents, and so on down the line for hundreds, if not thousands, of years.[1]

Though these genetic traits can be automatically installed, they can also be uninstalled, thanks to epigenetics, which, as Bruce Lipton[2] and others teach, offers us sway over our DNA through the power of our focused minds. The trick is to seek out these traits and dispositions and review them for their authenticity, veracity, and value for who we are now. Once revealed, we can eliminate those that no longer resonate with us and instead, choose ideologies and habits that do.

One of the hidden beliefs that lie deeply embedded in many of us is the idea that we cannot have direct contact with Source. The concept that an intermediary is essential for us to have a connection to what we think of as Divine has been passed along from generation to generation for millennia, and we often do not realize how cleverly disguised that belief can be. Of course, we understand that interpreters, teachers, guides, and even gurus are essential at crucial times in leading us along a spiritual path, yet, ultimately, we must grasp that it is in our human blueprint to have direct access to Source. This is especially true now that we understand that "we are the ones we've been waiting for." While we may mentally agree with this conclusion—in fact, it may even seem elementary—it is when direct contact occurs that the visceral *knowing* overtakes *believing*.

I remember my complete shock when one of my own buried beliefs was exposed.

I was startled when, on the day before Easter, 2011, Jesus

(who I call Yeshua), Mary Magdalene, and Mother Mary visited me for the first time in my office. I was stunned, first because I had never had visitations before, and second, because though I greatly admired Yeshua's teachings, I certainly did not have a close relationship with him. If anything, I had rejected formal religion and carried a righteous anger towards some of them for their restrictive natures and violent histories. Imagine my surprise, then, when my involuntarily response to Yeshua's presence was to shed tears of shame and unworthiness.

My mind raced: "Is this really happening? I am not worthy of the attention of these 'holy' beings (for that is how they *felt*)... Surely, someone more spiritually important should be receiving them instead!"

Wow. It is almost funny and even pitiful to remember this now, but it was very real and even scary for me at the time. The irony is that although I completely believed direct connection with the Divine was possible, when it happened to me, I panicked. I could not hold two conflicting beliefs: on the one hand, that I was unworthy, and on the other, the feeling that it felt so natural and personal, as though I was picking up where I had left off with those beloved beings who knew me inside and out.

It was a shock to realize that for my entire life I had been gazing at Source through a self-imposed, self-limiting glass ceiling I had no idea existed until that moment. I further recognized that this ceiling of unworthiness was a result of deep programming handed down for eons. As soon as I understood that *I* was the one disallowing this direct contact, there was a great evolutionary "shattering" of my being, and I opened fully to Source.

I am sharing this with you because we just do not know what foundational convictions are hiding deep within until we are confronted with new information. After the visit was over, I rooted out that ancient *incorrect* belief that special intermediaries were necessary to connect with Source and replaced it with my new knowing that direct contact was, and has always been, our God-given right. And we are all worthy, just as Yeshua taught.

Since then, I go directly to Source in my search for Truth, thanks in part to the heightened frequencies of the Infinity Wave, which I use to connect with higher consciousness quickly and easily, as described later. While it has been unnerving at times, my relationship with Yeshua and "the Mary's" has continued to flourish—what an education I have received from them! I truly do not know where I would be without their loving tutelage and guidance, especially whenever I was nervous to share with others whatever new information I had received. This channeling from my guides helped me immensely whenever I doubted what was happening to me and wondered how to move forward:

> "Living truth is like an arrow.
> It requires tremendous courage…
> It requires tremendous faith."

I do not feel the connection I have with those "holy" beings (and many other high-frequency visitors by now) makes me special in any way, and firmly believe that direct contact is available in an infinite variety of forms to every single human. It typically comes when least expected and is not something to be strived for as much as opened to. If you are ready to say, "I am a willing vessel," all that flows out of that statement will open you to Source above and the Divinity of the Earth. I also think that one of the best ways to get there is by using the Infinity Wave.

As you take that next step on your spiritual path, know that in going direct, you will be revealed to yourself and there will be many "enlightenments" in the meeting of obstacles and resistances. Using the Compassion and Love in the Wave to face and question the biases, untruths and other limiting beliefs embedded within your psyche will help you to wash them away, leading you to the ultimate truth that this is *your life*, and you get to choose your own beliefs and actions for the precious gift that it is, just waiting to be unwrapped.

Go direct—a magnificent realm awaits.

Source

Do you ever wonder what is pushing this evolution?

It is ridiculous to the point of being laughable to even attempt to describe Source, but I will share the miniscule amount that I have come to accept.

For me, it is more of a feeling than anything else. When I am in the presence of certain otherworldly wisdom, the sensation is extraordinary; there is an intensity and a calm at the same time. Most palpable, however, is the pervasive Love that uplifts the soul. It is wonderful beyond words and dependably available if we are open to it. I occasionally use "Divine" because *the feeling is divine!*

Another term I use for Source is "Creator Force" because on the brief but impactful occasions when I have been consciously visited by this energy, I encountered a combination of a singular Intelligence and an infinite, bursting, creative urge through which that Intelligence is expressed. When communing with Creator Force, it is as if I am conversing with that which is both immeasurably vast and yet so close to me that there is nowhere to hide and no need to do so. In the Bible, we are told that the only way to know God is through Yeshua, but that has not been my experience, nor has it been what he and Mary Magdalene have directly taught me. I understand now Yeshua's references to being like a curious child in our spirituality because a lovely innocence comes over me when having a chat like this one:

5-5-2015 (Creator Force arrives)

Hope*: Creator, please help me to understand more about the sentence: "You shalt love the Lord your God with all your heart and with all your mind and all your soul." Is this what you want from us humans?*

Creator*: You are allowed to love whatever you choose. I do not expect, nor do I <u>need</u> anyone's love, however, I do urge all Creation to experience love in all its facets. Love rolls throughout eternity and encompasses everything. Love is an engine that drives all things. Love is inherent in Creation. Humans are given the choice to love or not—that choice determines their* *experience on Earth.*

Hope*: Can you tell me more about you? Where do you come from? How were you created?*

Creator*: You would like to understand the mystery?*

Hope*: Am I able to understand it?*

Creator*: It is simpler than you might think. A flame exists because a spark combined with air. Later, a fire occurs when there is fuel added. I am the spark and the air and the fuel. I became this as a result of my own desire to know myself.*

Hope*: Did anything exist before you?*

Creator*: I don't know.*

Hope*: What's beyond the Universe? And beyond that?*

Creator*: A vastness you cannot imagine.*

Hope*: Does it behoove me to love you?*

Creator*: Only in that you may love yourself better through me, but it is not necessary. The most important thing is to love. It does not matter who or what you love—just love.*

Hope*: Creator, it is my understanding that we are not supposed to worship anyone—is that true?*

Creator*: Worship, no. Love and admire, yes.*

Hope: *Thank you so much for helping me to come to a modicum of understanding.*

Just like Creator Force wants to know Itself, we are encouraged to know ourselves, and the vehicle through which that can happen is Love. This push of evolution we are in is a way for us to evolve into closer relationship with our real natures as beings of Love and Light...As beautiful Godsparks, we are walking embodiments of Source.

A Brief Overview of Energy

"Everything is energy and that's all there is to it.
Match the frequency of the reality you want, and you
cannot help but get that reality."
~ Albert Einstein

"Energy" comes in various forms, some of which are easier to perceive than others. For instance, we can see the effects of fuel-based energy in the workings of a car engine—the fuel goes in, gets ignited and the resulting heat creates energy for the car to run. Electricity is a less tangible energy: it is derived from fuel, but we usually see only its *effects* (toaster, lamp, etc.). Though we cannot see the electricity itself, we can measure its presence around us all the time.

Likewise, we are inherently electrical beings and the Earth herself teems with electro-magnetic energy. The electrical energy in our bodies can be detected by EEG or EKG tests, which gauge the electrical output of the brain and heart, respectively. Acupuncture relies on energy channels within the body to create health and well-being. As I will discuss below, around the world there are thousands of standing stones, sacred rock geometries, and pyramids that act as giant acupuncture points to capture, hold, and broadcast telluric energies.

Then there is a more subtle life force energy flowing through all things known as Chi or Prana. I like this description by Esther Ekhart:

*"Chi energy is like a bridge between **your form,** which is your body, your thoughts, emotions, sensations, and **the formless** which is your essence, consciousness, awareness. In a way, when we trace chi back from form to formless, this is the journey of being on the spiritual path. First, there is the body, thoughts, emotions, sensations, etcetera, which could all be described as chi having come into form. Then, as part of your spiritual practice you learn to stop identifying with form and start feeling and identifying more with the inner body, with chi, pure life energy. Eventually, this will lead you back to your essence, which is pure awareness, the formless."* [3]

Yoga, Qigong, Tai Chi, and other practices use Chi as a guiding principle. Years ago, my guides introduced me to another life force energy called AMA (imagine it chanted rather than spoken), which they said is a more balanced feminine/masculine energy than Chi. (Go HERE to listen to the chant.)

Here is how they described AMA:

Archangel Abraham: *AMA emanates from above and*

25

below—it is a conduit like chi, but also has aspects of the feminine. It is more appropriate for the balance of the Masculine and Feminine. Both chi and AMA are currents of energy, but AMA is for now (these times). Kundalini is also life-force—again, we are talking about a subtle distinction. AMA carries more empathy, compassion, and love. The Infinity Wave is AMA and water (and other things, too difficult to understand). AMA and water can transmute anything, and the effects are far-reaching.

AMA is the life-force that is available to everyone. While it is generally thought of as feminine, it is a balanced blend of both energies. When you invite AMA into your field, you will be receiving a dose of pure Creation.

Hope: *How does the Infinity Wave fit with this?*

Abraham: *The Infinity Wave is a delivery system that can help to connect with a variety of energetics. It can be used to invite AMA in.*

Hope: *How will we know that AMA is within us?*

Abraham: *You will feel a sense of vitality and connectedness. AMA is here more openly now because it is a time for balance. AMA has always been present and has been called many things. Now it is time to speak openly about it.*

Thus, there are always unseen energies both within us

and around us. For millennia, healers of all kinds have been able to keenly sense, connect with, and focus these energetic pulses within the Earth, plants, animals, and people.

Even our ideas and emotions have quantifiable energy, as biologist Bruce Lipton wrote in *The Biology of Belief: Unleashing the Power of Consciousness, Matter and Miracles.* The conclusion that "thoughts are things" comes from those experiments and, more importantly, the *impact* that those thoughts can have upon our bodies and consciousness has profound consequences. In just one example, studies have shown that when a person is in the energy of fear, corrosive "fight or flight" hormones flood the body, lowering resistance to invading toxins.[4] Conversely, peace and safety are ideas that strengthen the immune system.

It is obvious why this dynamic relationship between our thinking and our bodies is so important to grasp at this time: if we are to boost our immunity by putting positive energy to work for us, then we must find ways to manage the anger, resentment, and frustration that threaten to destabilize us virtually every day. Using the Infinity Wave can help to restore a peaceful, non-judgmental mindset and to support our energy running freely.

Light

For countless ancient cultures, the Sun was understood as a sacred being and by extension, its Light was an emanation of Source. Worship was directed towards the Sun as a heavenly father that bestowed his bounty upon the land and people. One can easily see why such beliefs would last for millennia until science removed the veil of mystery, telling us that the bright thing in the sky was just a big ball of gas.

But is that really the whole story?

For many years, I not only took the Sun for granted, but, like most modern people, dutifully hid from it to avoid getting skin cancer. Sunshine had become a kind of necessary evil that we all had to contend with by using sunscreen, hats, and special clothing. And then, one summer evening as I led a group meditation while playing my "C" crystal bowl (tuned to the Solar Plexus), a golden light spilled into the room. I was mentally sending the Infinity Wave to all the participants when suddenly I was aware that the Sun—yes, THE Sun—was tapping me on the shoulder and wanted to talk. (Get your belief buckets out...)

To say I was surprised is an understatement—I was still unaccustomed to these unexpected communications and my mind wrestled with the idea that I might be hallucinating. However, the Sun was not to be denied and had two points to make...

First, "He" (for it was a masculine presence) was not happy about how humanity had not only forgotten Him but now vilified Him. Did we not understand His relevance to life and the Earth? These were not the protestations of a wounded ego but a sincere concern that we had gone way off course in our development as a species. If we were out of whack with the Sun, then naturally we would be out of whack with Nature. In an instant, I grasped what had been staring me in the face all along yet had not been obvious due to my conditioning: everything hinged on right relationship with the Sun!

Second, He showed me that His relationship with the feminine Earth was that of a loving protector. In grasping His magnificence, largesse, and desire to serve, I was chagrined to acknowledge my utter lack of understanding of how things really worked. Instantaneously, I deeply grasped the Sun cultures of yore and vowed to establish the proper bearing toward our star by Waving with it every day (the method will be explained later).

What I discovered during the ensuing Wave sessions with the Sun was that He would quickly come online with me and glow brighter to let me know He was sentient and aware of our connection. If I stayed longer than a few minutes in His embrace, however, I would drift into an altered state and become quite high—I never knew I could become drunk on sunlight! This made me realize that the Sun cultures of bygone days must have been operating in a bliss zone much of the time. No wonder they loved the Sun so much!

Modern recognition of the Sun's value can be understood via Sungazing, a practice of looking directly at the Sun at sunrise and sunset, when it is considered safe to do so. The biophotons emerging from the sunlight are thought to positively affect the optic nerve and the pineal gland, also known as our intuitive Third Eye. Other proven benefits are increased serotonin, melatonin, and Vitamin D levels, providing better moods and sleep, to name just a few. (I have found that Waving works just as well.)

As I learned from my friend, Peruvian shaman Jorge Luis Delgado, recognition of the Sun as a blessed benefactor is still alive and well in Andean shamanic cultures. They

believe that Light is intelligent, wise, and in service, just as
we are, and Jorge teaches that our first job every morning is
to connect with and honor the Sun in order to remember this.
He delineates four qualities of Light: Clarity, Transparency,
Warmth, and Brightness.[5]

In many current spiritual circles, increasing one's Light
is considered to be perhaps the most important element for
a soul's growth. After all, we were Light Beings before we
became embodied, and that Light is still essentially who we
are. Speaking simplistically, the idea is that Divine Light and
Divine Love are nearly synonymous, so if we can hold more
Light, we can hold more Love. Everything we do to increase
our capacity to glow more brightly enhances our evolution.

I am just scratching the surface here. There is much more
to be said about Light, but at least we have a platform now
for future conversation.

Resonance and Entrainment

*"All things in our universe are constantly in motion,
vibrating. Even objects that appear to be stationary
are in fact vibrating, oscillating, resonating, at
various frequencies. Resonance is a type of motion,
characterized by oscillation between two states. And
ultimately all matter is just vibrations of various
underlying fields."[6]*

Resonance can best be understood as a field of vibration.
Resonance explains why you feel happy in a group of like-
minded, loving people and out of sorts when you're with
those of a lower vibration.

To explain entrainment simply, if ten clocks of different sizes and varieties are on the same wall, eventually all the tic-toc's will come into sync with the one that has the strongest beat.

Even if you are not consciously aware of it, you are also in resonance with and entrained to the place where you live, whether a rural landscape or a bustling city. You can test this theory out by going to a completely different environment and seeing how long it takes to become resonant with the next location. I lived in New York City for many years, and upon leaving for vacation, it would take me at least three days to slow my rhythm down enough to resonate with the new environment. Living in a fast-paced place requires being in resonance with it just to survive, which I see as an expression of how wonderfully adaptive we are.

With this knowledge, we can make choices about with whom and where we wish to resonate. Having said that, sometimes we learn more from being in places and situations where we struggle. We can all look back on relationships with people or places we left behind because they just didn't fit with who we had become. My NYC days were full of challenges but also richness of experience. When it became clear that I had learned enough, I moved on to the next experience that was in better resonance for my next growth spurt. I wouldn't trade a moment of the struggles because of how they shaped and informed my evolution.

Dimensions

Even a casual discussion of dimensions needs to begin

with the understanding that they are non-linear, so any attempt to define them is necessarily limited by our ability to bring into linear language that which is beyond language. There are a multitude of varying opinions about the many dimensions and their characteristics, and I am not an expert on all of them, but I can briefly address the 3rd Dimension, which is what we live in here on Planet Earth, and the way 10D (the Infinity Wave) can impact it.[7]

From ancient mystics to modern science, we have been told that "reality" exists in many versions and that there are a multitude of dimensions beyond this one. With the exception of 1 and 2D, any dimension aside from 3D is non-material and, as a rule, each one has a faster, more refined frequency than the one before it. This beautiful world we agreed to inhabit operates under specific mandates of time, space, and gravity and exhibits a heavier density than those higher dimensions. Things here *appear* as solidly real because slowly moving atoms create dense objects. In the alternate realities with faster moving atoms, existence is much more fluid and malleable. You can visualize this by imaging a fan with blades that are clearly visible while still and even perhaps on the lowest setting. However, the faster the fan turns, the less we are able to perceive the blades, yet we know they are there. If the fan could go faster still, we may lose sight of the blades altogether.

We are told by many intuitive folks that 4D is the astral realm, where our emotional bodies and unconscious minds live. 5D represents a higher form of consciousness where we can experience Oneness, or Unity Consciousness, and is predicted by many spiritual leaders to be what we are evolving into as a species and a planet.[8] Though that reality might feel far away at the moment, I believe 5D is already accessible and, in fact, we are on the brink of a giant leap for humanity and the planet itself. But how will we get there from here?

Enter the Infinity Wave. It might be considered subtle at first, but when it is used more extensively, it becomes increasingly palpable. As a 10th dimensional energy, it carries within its watery flow a much purer vibration of Love and Compassion, energies that are usually too refined for us to experience here in 3D. However, when the Wave is invoked, its effect is to instantly elevate a given situation into a higher frequency.

One way to characterize 3D is its adherence to duality, the polarizing "rules of the game" here on Earth. For a visual metaphor, picture a large, grassy field with two posts fixed in the ground at opposite ends.

These posts represent duality: Yes/No, Either/Or, Right/Wrong, etcetera. The unconscious game that is played *ad infinitum* here on Earth is a struggled tug-o'-war between these two poles.

Five seconds on social media exposes vehement opinions both opposing and supporting whatever topic is put forth. In this resistant set-up, there is little access to creative solutions because the insistent driving force is to be RIGHT and to WIN—hence the pushing and pulling of the rope. Of course, this same locked-in game happens on both micro and macro scales—between individuals, between cultures, and between nations.

There is a good reason for this duality: *it makes us choose*, and that is what our evolution is all about. Each time we decide something, whether of high vibration or low, we identify ourselves more precisely with our higher selves and to Source. This is why we opted to come here in the first place—to exercise our options.

Over the last few decades, our societies have become increasingly divided and extreme in their opposition to one another, which is why the concept—and truth—that we are all One might seem far-fetched at this point. Because we cannot solve a problem from the place in which it was created, we must find ways to access a wiser, more refined, and imaginative point of view—we have got to get outside the struggle box.

To do this, imagine that the 10D Love and Compassion of the Infinity Wave hovers directly over this playing field, with the rounded loops of the "eight" wrapped around each of the posts.

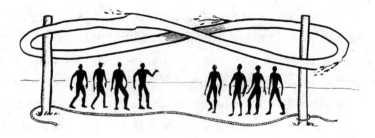

Yes, and...

As the watery infinity geometry flows, it is of such a high frequency that it disables 3D thinking and literally breaks up the game of resistance, replacing it with non-dual, non-linear thinking, thereby creating a blending of polarized positions.

Said another way, applying a 10th dimensional energetic to a 3D playing field elevates everything into a faster vibration in which struggle ("Either/Or") drops away and co-creation ("Yes, and...") with a higher intelligence becomes possible. If you try this, you will find that just by beginning to change your language, your whole perception shifts from linear thinking into multi-dimensionality.

The Infinity Wave co-creates change of all kinds by urging our awareness out of the literal, ego mind into a non-dual, co-creative Mind. The cool thing is that we do not need to try hard to achieve this—the Infinity Wave invites us to *allow* change, rather than *strive* to achieve it. Ultimately, the Wave stretches us to expand past our 3D mindsets, giving us *direct access to higher dimensions,* as discussed previously. Once we are no longer confined to 3D, we gain a wider perspective about how to be *in* the world but not *of* it. You see, the goal is not to escape this wonderful, juicy 3D reality, but to be freed from its dualistic rules, thus experiencing life in more fullness, freedom, and spaciousness.

Science uses terms such as the "quantum field" and "string theory" to describe the ever moving, inter-connectedness of all things, although such Oneness has been taught by spiritual leaders for millennia. The quantum field demonstrates that matter is fluid and changes when it is observed, which Einstein called "spooky action at a distance."

More recently, Lynne McTaggart—author of *The Power of Eight,* among other books—has conducted multiple experiments proving that reality shifts when exposed to concentrated thought.[9]

In its simplest form, the Infinity Wave allows us to observe what is; then, by applying it, shift that reality into something more desirable and of a higher vibration. When you invoke the Wave, you trust that the highest and best outcome will present itself for all involved—and that outcome may surprise you! This energetic is all about a supremely intelligent flow (a concept I will address later) so even if you have an idea about how a situation can be resolved, it might be too constrictive for the Wave. Trust is key here, and the acknowledgment that problem-solving from a 10th dimensional standpoint can look vastly different than what we would expect here in 3D.

It is mind-boggling to think that the simple application of an unspoken, imagined geometry could so immediately and profoundly alter 3D reality, yet this is exactly what happens. I have silently conjured the Wave countless times while in a difficult conversation, only to observe the tone of the argument gracefully shifting from combative to conciliatory. I have used it while traveling alone and with groups to help smooth and resolve every kind of snafu imaginable. I have employed it before surgery to ensure that all goes well. There are myriads of other ways to use the Wave—the possibilities are limitless.

Here is one inspiring example:

A woman friend was in City Hall awaiting her turn to have a clerk process her divorce papers. As she stood in line, she observed the generally cranky attitudes of all the clerks and the frustration levels of those needing their help. Because she had limited time in which to accomplish her goal and was worried that she might not have all her paperwork in order, she started to Wave the entire room to ensure that her process would go smoothly. When it was her turn, she stepped up to the counter and held her breath to see what would happen next. To her amazement, not only did her clerk become warm and engaging, but when they hit a snag in the paperwork, her clerk called others in for help, and soon all the clerks were happily collaborating to help this woman get her papers processed successfully!

This example shows how the Wave works within the quantum field. The woman's observation of City Hall dynamics offered her a choice-point, and she opted to rearrange reality for the best possible outcome through her intention and use of the Wave. In the process, the clerks also had a more joyful collaborative experience, and everybody won. Much like electrical energy, the Infinity Wave's 10th dimensional Love and Compassion may not be visible or easy to grasp with our minds, but we can certainly observe its effects and impact on behaviors.

Wave practitioners and I have sent Infinity Waves to doctors' offices, emergency rooms, courthouses, airports, and even Washington, D.C. to enhance communication and create smooth, flowing outcomes. In these instances, we envisioned Waves encompassing and/or hovering over the projected area like a ceiling fan. The possibilities are endless, as we will discuss later.

Sacred Geometry

"Sacred Geometry" is a term used to describe the idea that certain precise shapes and patterns recur throughout both the natural world and the Cosmos, giving rise to a belief that only a higher intelligence could have been designing Creation from the beginning.

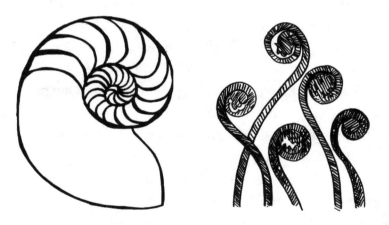

It is intriguing to contemplate that the building blocks of the material world—squares, triangles, circles, spirals and the more complex tetrahedrons and dodecahedrons—not only have specific symbolic meanings, but also frequencies.

Suffice it to say, these motifs are not accidental and there is plenty to unlock about them—subject matter for a different book!

To be brief, let us not think of geometry as static, two-dimensional scribbles on paper, but rather as a fully dimensional "living" entities. In her book, *The Alchemy of Nine Dimensions*, Barbara Hand Clow breaks down how Creation happens: a step-down vibrational process of light becoming sound, sound turning into geometry, and geometry into matter.

To learn more about the relationship between vibration (sound) and geometry, let us turn to a fascinating field: Cymatics. Studies have been done with substances such as sand or water and involve observing the impact of sound upon them. In the case of sand, a thin metal sheet holds a handful scattered randomly upon it. As ascending musical notes are played nearby, the metal vibrates and the sand moves from chaotic to increasingly complex geometries as the notes move higher in pitch. (You can find many YouTube videos on this.) I see this as a metaphor for our evolutionary process for we, too, move in and out of cohesive flow and chaos as we grow.

Furthermore, these geometries should be thought of as three-dimensional in nature—at minimum. For instance, instead of a circle, think of a sphere. In Freddy Silva's book, *Secrets in the Fields,* he urges the reader to see crop circles as a slice of the entire geometry, such as when an apple is split in half and we see the flat core even though we know full well that the apple is a 3-D thing.

Moving on, the geometry of infinity is called a lemniscate, a mathematical term representing the endless nature of infinity since it does not touch in the center crossing point but continues to circulate without ending, much like a circle with a twist.

My guidance has taught me that all of Life—past, present, and future—exists on the moving continuum of the lemniscate. For me, this is an easy way to imagine the concept that there is no time but Now, with everything happening all at once.

There are different versions of the mathematical infinity sign, but for our purposes, either upright or on its side, the Infinity Wave exemplifies balance, with both sections of equal size and in alignment. This continuum is the ultimate symbol of Unity, meaning that All is One. In spiritual evolution, we can employ the Infinity Wave first to become One within ourselves, followed by One with each other, One with Source, and One with all Creation. This Love, Compassion, and Unity consciousness is what is running when the Wave is invited into a person's consciousness.

Let us now investigate this geometry as it appears in the Flower of Life, an important symbol illustrating the creation of Life itself: the division of cells...

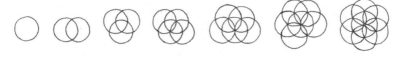

The repeated infinity signs embedded in this design imply that this dynamic geometry is essential to existence, while the overall pattern stresses the interconnectivity of all things.

This symbol's importance cannot be underestimated as it has been carved in antiquity into meaningful places around the world: under the paw of the lion that guards the Forbidden City in China, inside the Temple of Osiris, and even under some Roman roads, to name only a few.[10]

The Infinity Wave shape also demonstrates the ever-present expansion and contraction of Life: the watery flow moves through the narrowing center, or zero point, only to balloon into the wide circular part, and back again into the narrows, before repeating the journey of expansion and contraction, ad infinitum. This echoes the mighty, inescapable ebb and flow of Creation—our breathing expands and contracts, as do the tides and the seasons. Scientists such as Sean Carroll of C.I.T. theorize that the Universe itself will someday cease to expand as it is doing now and then will begin a contraction process called "The Big Crunch." Though it can feel uncomfortable when we're in the contraction phase (the peduncle), we have the comfort of knowing that any difficulties we face will inevitably shift with the flow of time. There is truth in the old adage, "This, too, shall pass."

As Above, So Below

Many of us have been taught to raise our vibrations upward, thinking that the faster and higher we go, the more enlightened we become. While this may be true, my understanding is that it is only part of the story.

In order to evolve in a balanced way, we must not only seek a rapport with the "Above," but also a connection with the "Below"—meaning with the conscious entity we call Earth.

It is the *combination* of the two that brings a more complete evolution for our species.

You can think of the process of evolving as two spirals, one moving upwards and another moving downwards into the Earth.

The Earth (also referred to as Gaia) is a conscious being, and when we chose to be born here we were given a birthright to be *with* the planet in every sense. Just imagine the simplest thing: as our feet engage with the soil of the earth, we simultaneously discharge our built-up negative charge and are fed with a positive electrical charge. (Nowadays, we can achieve this through "Earthing" materials that simulate this connection for those who have lost the interest or ability to pursue it naturally.)

Taking this a step further, the consciousness of Earth invites us to empty whatever does not serve us—physically, mentally, emotionally, and spiritually—down into Her, where She willingly transmutes it into something more useful and beautiful. It's like a giant composting process, and, as you will see, the Infinity Wave comes in handy.

Of course, these are not new ideas to indigenous people, who have always known how sentient the Earth is, have never lost their connection to Her, and continue to honor Her as the Mother of Life. Many of us who have been disconnected from our indigenous roots are trying to catch up by relearning various skills, such as sensitivity to the electromagnetic currents that make up the grid running within and around the planet. These currents were used in ancient times to navigate, establish dwellings, create ideal planting areas, and identify power spots for healing, fertility, and worship.

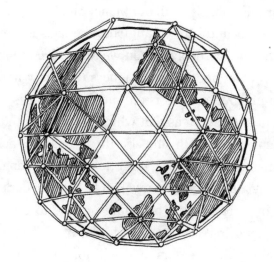

Some of these grid intersections were identified by huge standing stones that were inserted into the soil like acupuncture needles in order to transmit the heightened Earth energy to the surrounding fields. Scientific studies have proven that crops planted where these stones exist are more fertile and abundant than fields without the broadcasting stone.[11]

This one small example of tapping into telluric energies gives a hint of how much there is to discover once we begin to deepen our relationship with our planet, the living being with which we are beautifully entangled, who asks nothing from us yet gives so generously. When we recognize the abundant power within Her and Her willingness to deeply nourish us, we start to grasp that there is an interaction that is every bit as important and loving as that which we have with Source.

Communication with the Earth is readily accessible and yet many of us have forgotten how to enable this conversation. I invite you to awaken to the wonders that the Earth has in store for you by going outside to observe Her greatness, honoring Her as you do so. You will feel your heart becoming tied to Hers, and will long to do everything in your power to preserve Her.

This leads us to recognize the unique position that we humans hold in this grand landscape of Heaven and Earth. Although Source and the unseen Masters carry the ultimate wisdom, they are not embodied and can only work through us for their highest ideals to become reality here on Earth.

Likewise, the Earth has plants and trees and animals living upon Her, but only we humans can take action and speak on Her behalf. This is an awesome place of honor that we have each been gifted with; I believe that we humans are the conduits for the Above and Below, and as such, we are the only ones who can consciously play out what they tell us is best and highest for ourselves, for our communities, and for the Earth.

How can we begin to create such a communication? Try imagining an Infinity Wave extending itself down into the Earth under your feet, crossing at your belly button and wrapping high above your head to give you the sense of being a walking conduit. In this way, you are always carrying Earth's and Heaven's spiritualities within your field. As conduits, wherever we walk, we create change.

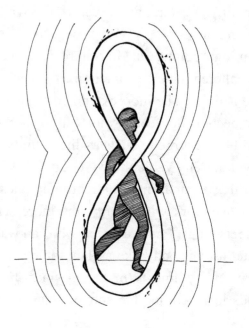

Altered States

In an altered state, our consciousness steps outside the bounds of regular daily reality. Even without the aid of spiritual substances like psychedelics, we unknowingly go in and out of altered states quite often. For a dramatic example, remember the intoxication you felt when in the throes of a new love and the world looked fresh and sparkling? Same world, altered you. Similarly, when a beloved is suddenly gone, you might enter a vulnerable realm in which everything feels tentative and oddly transparent, like there are holes in the Universe. Same world, altered you.

When these emotional tsunamis hit, reality looks completely different from one day to the next because our heightened feelings have altered our perceptions. These altered states go by other names: "down in the dumps," "floating on air," et cetera, and it can take a while to come "back down to Earth."

Daydreaming, "zoning out" in Nature, and meditation are more subtle altered states, characterized by an increase in Alpha wave activity. The more we practice them, the more attuned we become to feeling not fully "in this world." Working with an energetic such as the Infinity Wave can instantly invoke an enjoyable altered state of gentle relaxation, which then often expands into a delightful lightness of being.

The more we work with energy, the more sensitive we are to its effects on us. I have a friend who can walk through the forest and use his body like a giant tuning fork to sense where every energy line is in the ground—he needs no dowsing rods to determine the subtle dynamics happening in the Earth. I believe early humans all had this capacity, so it makes sense to me that, with practice, we can reawaken it within ourselves.

What Does Water Have to Do with It?

Water is the essence of life, without which we would soon perish. Depending on our age, 70 to 90% of our bodies are water. It is a medium that not only exists everywhere, including outer space, but mysteriously can morph into three distinct forms: fluid, frozen, and gaseous. Scientists still do not fully comprehend it because nothing else acts in this way.

In Nature, water has a calming, enlivening influence on our nervous systems, which is one of the reasons so many people prefer to live near it. Liquid water can restore hydration, remove obstacles, carve a path of least resistance, and cleanse just about anything.

Water even has memory and consciousness. As has been shown in recent years, water can undergo molecular change simply by being exposed to a printed word, expressed idea, or transmitted thought. Dr. Masaru Emoto and others proved that water molecules became beautifully crystalline in shape in response to loving words, while molecules exposed to negative words turned into dark, chaotic blobs. The same is true for water that is thanked rather than criticized. Brackish ponds have come back to life, thanks to the meditations of a single monk.[12]

This scientific proof that water responds to ideas has profound ramifications for our understanding of consciousness. Knowing that water shapeshifts in response to subtle frequencies raises such questions as: "What happens to the water in our bodies when we hear mean words or harsh music, or watch violent entertainment?" Conversely, imagine the impact upon the water in our bodies when we flood ourselves with the Love and Compassion of the Infinity Wave!

As we know, water can have many 'personalities,' from a calm trickling brook to an eighty-foot, powerful ocean wave. Likewise, I have experienced the water in the Infinity Wave sometimes as gentle, embracing cleansing agent for the body and spirit, and other times as a forceful "mover and shaker" if energies are particularly stuck. The Wave can become any of water's many forms.

Flow States

To get a sense of how flow states work, first imagine yourself being internally stuck, unable to move forward no matter how hard you try. Life is a struggle of pushing and pulling, with little forward progress.

Now, imagine you are floating down a gentle river, not swimming but instead allowing the water to pull you along, this way and that, with no conscious destination in mind. A peacefulness presides as you trust the river to deliver you safely to a new shore. In this state, you are not taking charge, but accepting the wisdom of the river to direct your journey.

This is being in a flow state, in which life becomes less about struggle and more about ease, less about certainty and more about discovery, less about attainment and more about receptivity. The Infinity Wave helps to sustain this state, melting away resistance and introducing a tranquil willingness to trust an invisible guidance system.

You might wonder what happens to your own initiative in such a scenario. Being "in flow" requires a willingness to be guided *and* an ability to choose a course of action from an intuitive place, not solely from the mind. This is what I would call "co-creation," a combination of being led and acting upon the information delivered while in the flow state.

I have so many examples of this because it is how I have come to live my life, but I'll give you just one…

Every year, I work with my etheric guide team to put together a group trip to a powerful place in the world. After dowsing for where and when I should go, I start planning, always leaving plenty of space for the unexpected once we get there. After a dozen of these travels to far-reaching places, I've learned that when I say "Yes" to the parameters that the guides provide and include the Infinity Wave, the trip always unfolds in beautifully serendipitous ways, leading us elegantly and smoothly into experiences that we could never have imagined. The bonus is that I never feel alone when conducting journeys because I trust that the guides will provide exactly what the group needs.

In this way, the co-creation is a combination of being in flow with the guide team and taking the initiative to follow through, all under the gentle auspices of the Infinity Wave. The best thing about this set-up is that I no longer carry the heavy weight of worry as I venture forth. Instead, I look forward with anticipation at what will unfold, knowing that it will be perfection for all. This approach has never failed me.

Endnotes

1. https://www.theatlantic.com/health/archive/2018/10/trauma-inherited-generations/573055/)

2. Lipton, Bruce. The Biology of Belief. Hay House, 2015.

3. Ekhart, Esther. https://www.ekhartyoga.com/articles/practice/what-is-chi

4. https://www.health.harvard.edu/staying-healthy/understanding-the-stress-response

5. See Delgado, Jorge. Andean Awakening. Millichap, 2012 and Inca Wisdom: 5 Return to Joy. Sirio Eirl, 2020.

6. Hunt, Tam. Scientific American, 2018; Jepsen,Kathryn. Symmetry Magazine, 2013.

7. For more about dimensions, see Clow, Barbara Hand. The Alchemy of Nine Dimensions. Hampton 7 Roads, 2011/2012.

8. For more intuitive leaders, consider following astrologer Pam Gregory, Laura Eisenhower, and virtually every presenter on Gaia TV.

9. See McTaggart, Lynne. The Power of Eight: Harnessing the Miraculous Energies of a Small Group 9 to Heal Others, Your Life, and the World. Atria Books, 2017.

10. You can see it in its 3D form here: https://www.youtube.com/10 watch?v=c2itA0q-cU8

11. See Silva, Freddy. Secrets in the Fields. 11 Hampton Roads, 2002.

12. See Emoto, Masaru. The Hidden Messages in Water. Simon 12 and Schuster, 2004.

1. https://www.theatlantic.com/health/archive/2018/10/trauma-inherited-generations/573055/)

2. https://www.theatlantic.com/health/archive/2018/10/trauma-inherited-generations/573055/)

3. https://www.theatlantic.com/health/archive/2018/10/trau-

THREE
how to begin
with the infinity wave

"The power of imagination makes us infinite."
~ John Muir

The Infinity Wave is an energetic gift from a loving Universe to help us evolve more easily and smoothly into the next level of reality as multi-dimensional beings. When invited in, the Wave delivers an inner sense of harmony, flow, and stability. It is surprisingly easy to use, and the good news is, there is no wrong way to do it. Really.

The only requirement is imagination. As Einstein said, "Imagination is more important than knowledge, for knowledge is limited whereas imagination embraces the entire world, stimulating progress, giving birth to evolution."

Though we have been conditioned to disregard imagination as untrustworthy or insignificant, nothing could be further from the truth. To me, imagination and inspiration are inter-changeable terms to describe the pure conduits through which Source communicates with us in unlocking the doors to Creation. It is a vital force and a divinely given tool inherent in the human design—it is our connection to the worlds beyond this one.

Did the great works of art and music come solely from human minds, or was there a collaboration between the artist and Source? I think the latter is true, and it explains why the ancient Greeks and Romans routinely called upon the appropriate muse to support them when pursuing any creative endeavor. Among copious examples of this divine connection is Frederick Handel, who reportedly wept for joy as he felt God pouring through him while he penned the music for the *Hallelujah Chorus* in a single night.[1]

Imagination is a unique form of energy, for where thoughts go, energy flows. Look around your room—everything within view began in someone's imagination. Ideas are regularly plucked from an imagined realm to become real in this dimension. Lynne McTaggart has shown how collective imagination dramatically and reliably impacts and shifts the material world.[2]

Group consciousness is not required to influence our own bodies, however. Recent studies of the placebo effect prove the power of the conscious mind to effect healing.[3] Studies have also shown that merely by conjuring up a beautiful, natural scene in one's mind, heart rates, and breathing are consistently lowered.

It is easy to see how imagination also impacts our beliefs. When we encounter proof that reality can be altered "merely" by ideas, we then have to expand our beliefs about how malleable reality actually is, which then sets up a cascade of possibilities for consideration. Imagination helps us solve problems from a place beyond where they were created, which is why it is crucial to our very survival.

For those who think you do not visualize well, please be patient and do not give up. Because modern society often downplays imagination, many people have not had a chance to develop it and are insecure about not being able to visualize easily. Though quite a few participants in my workshops have felt that way initially, sooner or later the Wave imagery unexpectedly popped into their awareness in vivid ways.

One participant admitted on the second day of a workshop that he had never been able to visualize anything besides blackness, and this was causing a mixture of frustration and disappointment during our practices. Not only did he excitedly report the very next day that the Wave had appeared to him, but a week later a design for his new logo that he had been struggling with dropped into his mind in full color and detail! The Wave had helped his imagination to kick back in.

Be compassionate with yourself as you start playing with the Wave imagery, and you will find that it *wants* to show up and dance in your life.

The Daily Wave

There are an unlimited number of ways to use the Infinity Wave, and I will suggest some to start with below. The Daily Wave, for example, is a great way to start playing with Wave energy, as it is meant to enhance everyday life so that everything goes more smoothly.

Applying the Infinity Wave to your day can be done at whatever pace is most comfortable for you. Much like any other spiritual technique such as yoga, the practice continues to deepen the more experience you have with it. Being in Wave energy helps to loosen mental constraints of limited possibility and open to the unknown. Each time one layer of limitation is resolved, there is another layer of freedom to be addressed—you can work with it endlessly to create specific, as well as general, changes. This is the process of conscious evolution.

The Infinity Wave instructions offered here are merely guidelines for a daily practice, for each user is encouraged to personalize the Wave for themselves—what might work for me, may not be the absolute best application for you, AND these applications may change with each situation. Remember that because the Wave is non-dual (no right or wrong), so *you truly cannot do it incorrectly*. Call upon the Wave, trust your intuition, and let it guide you into a rich dialogue with this living energetic. When your reality begins to shift, as it surely will, you will gain confident excitement witnessing how this 3D dualistic world transforms into expanded, joyful, Unity consciousness.

It takes a while to create a new habit, so to encourage staying in Wave energy, I suggest printing out small images of it and sticking them in places you are likely to spend time (bathroom mirror, kitchen fridge, car dashboard, work cubicle or computer, etc.). Try using the Infinity Wave while doing activities such as:

- Cooking
- Driving
- Working
- Shopping

- Doctor visits
- Relating with family and friends, etc.

Whenever you are in Wave energy, you are bathing yourself in Love and Compassion, bringing your heart rate down, and staying in equilibrium. No matter what you are doing, your day will flow easily and without stress when you invite the Wave to dance with you.

The Wave in the Heart

I always recommend experiencing the Infinity Wave first in the heart.

After establishing some deep breathing, simply imagine a small Infinity Wave floating in your heart center (you can use your finger to trace the shape over your heart if that helps to get the imagery going). The infinity shape can be vertical or horizontal and can appear as two-dimensional or as a three-dimensional hourglass. *Picture the water flowing in the "8" geometry.*

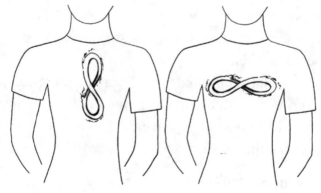

Though it might be easier at first to see it as blue, it may appear to you in any color. Likewise, it can be moving at any pace that feels comfortable in the moment. Pay close attention to how your heart feels with that image floating there—do you sense a slight tug, movement or softening in your heart center? Are you breathing more deeply and feeling calmer?

As you allow the Wave's tremendous Love and Compassion to flow throughout your heart, receive its blessing for your choice to come into this lifetime to be here for the massive changes that are afoot. We are usually bereft of this level of acknowledgment, like dry sponges deeply in need of spiritual hydration. Feel your worthiness as the Infinity Wave bathes you in appreciation for all you have done to exemplify love along your path so far. You are infinitely seen, heard, and loved. The Infinity Wave extends the invitation to a non-egoic self-love, a step many skip over in their spiritual journey even though it is a crucial component in the ability to love others fully. "Love thy neighbor as thyself..." requires that we first kindly accept ourselves, "warts and all."

If you do not experience any sensations, no worries— there are no "should's" or "shouldn't's" with the Infinity Wave. However, the more you use it, the more evidence you will observe in its effects.

It really is that simple and easy. There are more complex applications that I will discuss later, but in the beginning, it is enough to just invite the Wave energy into your heart and notice even the tiniest shifts that might occur.

The Wave in the Body

The Infinity Wave is pliable and can be any size, from

microscopic to galactic. Once you have a sense of the Wave in your heart, allow it to slowly stretch and lengthen into your torso as you breathe, eventually moving up through the lungs to the base of the neck and down through the abdomen to the sacrum. The crossing point might be at the solar plexus or at the heart—your choice. Notice again the color and pace of flow, and what effect, if any, this moving water might be having on your body.

Once you can feel the Infinity Wave flowing within you, experiment with the pace of flow—speed it up until it rushes like a spring brook, then slow it down to a gentle, bubbling trickle. Observe the different effects these speeds have within your body and settle on one that feels most natural and comfortable for the current moment. You may employ the Wave in your body to help you sleep, realign, balance, and/or cleanse your inner self.

Shifting Emotional States

During (or after) an upsetting situation or conversation, you can place a Wave wherever you hold your distress. For example, since it is common to hold anger in the abdomen, imagine a Wave of appropriate size in the belly, and let the water run very quickly like a rushing spring river. You should immediately notice a softening of your emotional state, which might bring in a new perspective and/or a fresh idea about how to resolve the issue, and perhaps even humor, as I described before. This can take a few seconds or several minutes, depending on your focus.

I remember one instance when I was in a heated

conversation with one of my teenage children. Rather than becoming further enraged, I removed myself to my bedroom to calm down, and immediately started to run a rushing, powerful Wave in my abdomen where my anger was brewing. As I closed my eyes and concentrated on the Wave in my gut, I spontaneously felt a physical melting and relief spread throughout my body. Then, a little window opened in my mind's eye, and a film-like replay of the previous argument appeared.

While still focusing on the Wave, I "watched" and noticed the ways in which I had contributed to the escalation of the conversation; I then "saw" how I could respond differently going forward. Next, I viewed what I needed to say in order to repair the relationship, and, finally, I found myself laughing over the absurdity of it. When I opened my eyes, my body was calm and I was in a light-hearted mood, ready to patch things up.

I thought I must have been there for half an hour or so, but the clock read that only five minutes had passed! This was the moment I recognized that the Infinity Wave has a tremendous ability to shift emotional states very quickly back into a "flow state." Imagine if we all did this every day!

Relief from Pain

The Infinity Wave has proven to be quite effective for physical pain. Remember, there is no wrong way to use it, so allow yourself full freedom to explore what works best for you. You can try using a single Wave or multiples, making them any size and pace, and placing them wherever you have pain. For chronic pain, simply activate the Wave like turning on a light switch in that area, allowing it to operate continually in the background. If more acute pain occurs, try focusing intently on a swiftly moving Wave in the troubled area—this may take a few minutes or quite a bit longer, depending on your familiarity with the Wave and the degree of pain.

One testimonial I received was from a woman who typically had three-day migraines that would land her in bed. When she felt one coming on, she applied the Wave and three hours later was pain-free. In the process, she learned a great deal about her beliefs and gained a spiritual perspective that empowered her for the future.

As a Communication Tool

You can apply the Infinity Wave to relationships or challenging situations. Because it is primarily comprised of Love and Compassion, it cannot harm another person. On the contrary, it can be beneficial to relationships of every kind since 10D energetics release everyone from 3D duality, thereby delivering an overall sense of freed-up well-being, peace, and connectedness. Best of all, thanks to the geometry, the Love and Compassion inherent within it naturally returns to the sender; what you send is what you get!

When the Wave is called into conversations of all kinds, both near and far, you will be amazed at how easily the discourse flows, how smoothly differences are resolved, and how open your heart feels during these interactions. Try it on the phone or online and just have fun with it—it's truly miraculous.

If you anticipate having a difficult conversation with someone, apply the Wave ahead of time to that person or to the room where you will meet. I think you will find that the conversation flows more smoothly and positively, with happier outcomes. This has happened to me so many times that I have lost track and I know that it's been true for many other Wave users.

Imagine all the places in your life that are worrisome, troubling, or uncertain and simply overlay the Wave on each of those situations or relationships. Then stand back and watch what happens.

The Wave can be taught very quickly to people of all ages. Whether you try it out with a loved one or a stranger, you can decide whether you want to share with them that you are using this technique. *If both people are consciously running the Wave, then the positive effects are multiplied!*

Between Two People in Close Proximity:

Imagine that one end of the "8" loop is attached to your heart center and the other end is in the heart center of someone you care about. Then, "run" the Wave between your hearts while looking into one another's eyes. Feeling the current of that infinity geometry moving through you, away from you, and toward you once again, you will understand that this energetic carries a powerful connectivity.

As you focus your attention on the flowing Wave, you may begin to feel movement or even a slight tug within your heart center. As this is happening, notice any shifts that might be occurring in the interaction you are having: there could be a softening of facial expression or body stance, a lightening of tone or increased gentleness.

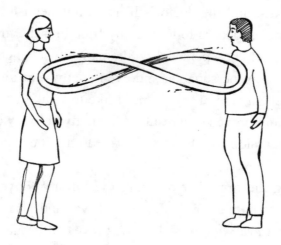

If you're working the Wave with a stranger, such as a check-out clerk or bank teller, start Waving while you are in line and see what happens when it is your turn to pay; it might surprise you to see a smile appear where there had been none before.

Along with other Wave practitioners, I have witnessed one-hundred-eighty-degree shifts in a nano-second. One of my favorite stories is about the anesthesiologist who was not demonstrating any bedside manner toward her patient, a friend of mine who was heading into a potentially dangerous surgery. During the pre-surgical inquiry, the doctor was extremely cold and did not make any eye contact with her patient while robotically firing off medical questions. I could see my friend becoming worried because she understandably wanted to feel safe and cared for by this doctor.

I lightly thought, "I do not like this picture. I'd like another one, please." Immediately, a forceful Wave blasted from my solar plexus, and the doctor's head simultaneously popped up from her clipboard to look at my friend for the first time. In an instant, her personality dramatically changed—she became warm, personable, and even chatty, and ultimately took excellent care of my friend. I like to think that her day was much improved as a result of the hefty delivery of Love and Compassion that helped her rise to a better version of herself.

During the first year of using the Infinity Wave, I was surprised to notice how judgmental I was and, in fact, how judgmental *everyone* was. This was revealed because when we would wave one another, the hierarchical playing field automatically leveled out—there was no agenda and no levels, just pure, equal, human-to-human connection in Love and Compassion. When I wasn't Waving, I observed how my usual thought patterns would drift back to identifying likes and dislikes, which basically added up to judgment of everything. I realized that the very first step in my new evolutionary journey would be to shift out of judgment into acceptance and love. If I had a bumpy issue with someone, I simply invited the Infinity Wave in to smooth my inner waters and bring me back to equanimity.

I also began to see the difference between judgment and discernment. Judgment emerges from a hierarchical, dualistic, "I'm better than you" perspective, whereas discernment sits more cleanly energetically and does not make anyone or anything "less than" in the choosing process.

In the words of Steve Nobel, *"....Judgment is about good and bad... Discernment is about usefulness."* In the story I just told about the anesthesiologist, I was surprised and pleased that after a year of working with the Wave, my desire for a different picture carried no burden of blame on the doctor. In fact, it carried great compassion for her. I could tell that I had evolved, thanks to the wisdom of the Wave.

Between Two People at a Distance:

Just as with someone in close proximity, you can propel an Infinity Wave out to anyone you wish. Picture the recipient as you connect with them heart-to-heart with the Wave, or you may imagine that they are held head-to-toe in it. As you begin the process of "waving" your person, you may notice that suddenly the Wave has taken a different color or positioning than what you had originally imagined. This kind of interplay brings more awareness of the *living* aspects of this energetic—it often knows better than we do about what is in the highest good of all. The Wave always presents itself in the form most needed by that person. Accept it with gratitude for the intelligence that guides it.

Connection with Nature and Grounding:

One of my favorite uses of the Infinity Wave is strengthening my connection with the natural world. It has become increasingly clear to me that developing this relationship is essential if we are to survive, let alone thrive.

What would it take to re-establish a consistently loving contact with our Gaia?

By simply Waving with Nature, a relationship is established and can flourish. When we consider that virtually every aspect of Nature has consciousness, the Waving possibilities are endless. Gone is the illusion of separation when we can unite through the loving, compassionate flow of the Wave with any tree, animal, rock, plant, body of water, mountain, canyon, or star.

I have tested this connection with my dowsing rods and carried on many a conversation with natural elements, although rods are not needed for communication. The Earth has a way of conversing with us in symbols, if we have but eyes to see and ears to hear. Much of the discourse is subtle, but She constantly sends us signals, which we sometimes fail to notice or understand. Shamans are helpful in deciphering the messages, but each of us is quite capable of developing our own language with Her as we build the relationship.

It is critically important to be able to ground quickly and easily in order to stay stabilized during tumultuous times. Stabilization does not just mean rooting into the Earth—it means being clearly aligned to above (Source and Light) and to below (Earth). As I have discussed, the geometry of the Infinity Wave is a perfect representation of those equally spiritual realms.

While breathing deeply, imagine that you have your feet on the ground standing within a giant Infinity Wave with its loops moving six feet down into the Earth and equally above your head. If you want to experiment further, perhaps the bottom of the "8" wraps around the core of the Earth while the top half shoots up into space. You can choose where the center crosses, either at your solar plexus or your heart. As the watery energetic runs and you continue to breathe, you will feel yourself connected to everything in an unshakeable, yet flowing, joyful way. Try this with bare feet on the ground or a rock to really feel "plugged in."

This practice can be done even if you are living in a busy city and want to slow your rhythm down. Simply find yourself a patch of green to sit or lie on and begin to breathe with the Earth beneath you while running a Wave as described. This will help you gain more mastery over creating and accessing the pulse that is best for you, no matter how cacophonous the environment is.

It is also very helpful and nourishing to Wave with water. The ocean sends and receives both information and light from the Earth to the Sun in a constant communication, so a Wave of love for the ocean touches every shore and beyond. Waving with any water will enhance it—even a puddle, the sink, or a snow field. Caution: I once Waved with Niagara Falls, which was so powerful that I almost got pulled over the side of the boat!

Endnotes

1.   https://www.udiscovermusic.com/classical-features/13 handel-messiah/ "Handel composed Messiah in just 24 days without getting much sleep and or eating much food. While writing the 'Hallelujah' chorus Handel's servant discovered him with tears in his eyes and he exclaimed, "I did think I did see all Heaven before me, and the great God Himself seated on His throne, with His company of Angels."

2.   See McTaggart, Lynne. The Power of Eight: Harnessing the Miraculous Energies of a Small Group to Heal Others, Your Life, and the World. Atria Books, 2017.

3.   See https://www.shiftfrequency.com/the-placebo-effect/.

FOUR
the deeper dive
nine practices for individual and collective transformation

Now that we have explored the Daily Wave, the next step is to delve into the transformative practices designed to give you a leap forward on your spiral of conscious spiritual evolution. Each of the nine practices came as a surprise, and only when looking back did I understand the brilliance and sequence of their messages.

Although I will briefly outline each practice below, they are ultimately meant to provide a powerful experience through the medium of sound (crystal bowls) and spoken word, so I strongly urge you to listen to them. I will provide the first two practices as a gift—the rest can be purchased for a nominal sum.

I also highly recommend that you work your way slowly through them in the order in which they are presented because the Higher Intelligence that sent them created an experiential road map for spiritual evolution that deepens with every step. Please do not rush through, but savor them, being sure to fully integrate each one before moving to the next. This can take days or weeks and may involve replaying the practice until you feel complete.

Once you have completed all of these practices, the Infinity Wave will be so embedded in your system that you won't be able to live without it. Your life will already have taken on this evolutionary quality, and it will continue to play out as time goes forward. You can trust in that.

For all the practices, I suggest that you sit in a comfortable chair as opposed to lying down, when there is always the potential that you will fall asleep.

Each meditation begins with deep Pranic breathing. (Prana is the Sanskrit word for "breath of life.") This method of deep breathing facilitates a connection to the Earth and Source, while simultaneously fueling the body with oxygen. As enlivened breath, it is an essential component of the Wave work.

Pranic Breathing

Here is a simplified version of how to do Pranic breathing:[1]
Visualize a tube extending from your crown (top of head)

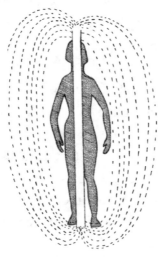

down through your sacrum at the base of your spine. This is your pranic tube.

Begin in your heart center by deeply exhaling through your Pranic tube down into the Earth, emptying any heavy energies that may be in your field. Then, take a deep inhalation up from the Earth into your heart center, allowing the Earth energy, the life force of Mother Gaia, to flow up into your heart. Each exhale takes you deeper into the Earth, while each inhale expands your heart with all the Earth has to offer you. Do this until you feel a deep connectedness with the Earth.

Now deeply exhale from your heart center and upward through the crown, expanding like a fountain into the Cosmos above and around you. Then, inhale that energy into your heart center, feeling its light. Each exhale expands you outward, while each inhale activates the cosmic life force within you and helps you to embody your spiritual essence. Do this until you feel connected to the cosmic energies.

Now, do them both at the same time, simultaneously drawing in Prana from below and above straight into your heart, and exhaling in both directions. (This can take some practice.) Feel your heart expanding and the complete balance that is created as you are connected to the realms of Source and the Earth.

The Nine Original Infinity Wave Practices

To experience the first two practices for free and gain access to the other practices, please use this QR code

Practice 1: Introduction to the Infinity Wave

Despite being quite short, this first practice will deliver your first felt sense of the Wave and leave you with a delightful peace and ease.

Practice 2: The Infinity Cradle

Now that you've experienced the power of the Wave to soften and expand your heart, let us explore its watery nature and how it can be used within and around the body. The Infinity Cradle practice offers a variety of opportunities and applications, one of which is to shake us free from the density of 3D through a brief disconnection from Gravity.

Another is to experience its water as a cleansing element. As the watery flow of the Infinity Wave moves through your physical, emotional, mental, and spiritual bodies, it re-establishes equilibrium while removing resistances and blocks, bringing a new sense of peace and ease. You may need to turn up the velocity of the watery flow from time to time, especially if you run up against some particularly stubborn beliefs, and you may also find that the color of the Wave needs to change according to the situation. As I said, please make it your own; the Wave is yours to explore. It really is the change that makes change easier.

The Infinity Cradle is also a great way to maintain Wave energy throughout the day. Instead of the mental chatter of worrying over situations that you cannot control, sustaining a Wave "state" disengages you from whatever hampering emotions are flowing through you and frees your mind to be receptive to new information and solutions. When negative emotions become less entangled, your heart and mind can work in a beautiful synchrony, much like having a handyperson take care of all the business you would rather not have to deal with while you process at a higher level.

I particularly like using the Infinity Cradle for invoking sleep, when going to bed as well and if I awaken during the night. Try it and see!

Practice 3: Body Appreciation

Addressing appreciation for the physical body often rings alarm bells because most of us have been profoundly discontented with our bodies for much of our lives. Sadly, in our culture we have been led down a road of extreme self-criticism about how we look; we're too this, or too that... and social media has only exacerbated this harsh perspective.

Many years ago, I had my own issues with body disgust, so I understand this topic very well. Working with the Wave brought me into a newfound resonance with my body through Love and Compassion, and from there I started to understand that our bodies are one with our beloved planet. Not only is our chemistry similar to the Earth's, but our electrical energy fields are interlaced with Hers. On both physical and spiritual levels, we are Her children—there is no separation. Therefore, when we are critical and punishing of our bodies, by extension we are critical and punishing of the Earth.

When I first grasped this concept, I was dismayed to remember all the times I had bemoaned my waistline or thighs or whatever was not quite perfect. It hurt to think that by expressing harshness towards myself, I was doing the same towards the Earth. Of course, I would *never* speak that way to Her, so from that moment on I honor and thank my body because I maintain honor and gratitude for the Earth.

This practice will help to quiet that critical voice and move you into compassion and appreciation for the magnificent home you walk around in. It literally is a wonder; no matter what size or what abilities or inabilities, your body continues to function and serve you in ways that you might not think about or adequately acknowledge. I hope you emerge from this experience feeling much more positive about your Earth suit.

Practice 4: Swim in the Earth

This practice was a complete surprise when it dropped in, and only afterward did I grasp the import of it. In this meditation, you will be taken on a journey deep into the Earth where you will keenly feel Her pulse as your pulse and emerge with a more profound appreciation of Her inner realms. When I came out of this practice for the first time, I was more in love with Gaia than ever—I hope the same holds true for you!

Practice 5: Time Travel

We are told that we are bound here in 3D life through Time, Space, and Gravity. You have already had the experience of being released from Gravity in the Infinity Cradle and felt how wonderfully freeing that was. Now we will explore being released from Time.

We think of Time as being linear, as if the past, present, and future happen on an endless line stretching forwards and backwards. Many scientific and spiritual minds have suggested that all Time is happening simultaneously, which is congruent with the lessons from the Infinity Wave.

What if we had a way to disconnect from Time, even for a short while? Some people are wary of disengaging from linear Time because, in a sense, it is the thread that weaves us all into this matrix. So, we are going to practice this experience in an entirely safe environment, and you will feel for yourself how wonderfully free you can be when detached from Time.

As the Infinity Wave sweeps you along, you will discover that Time is a wave that you can ride and adjust, and not a linear mechanism that holds you fast. You will also learn how to stretch Time and move it backward or forward. As you do this, you will come to a visceral understanding that 3D life is not all that is available to us as spiritual beings, but the mere tip of the iceberg.

Practice 6: Power Cell

Did you know that you can charge yourself up as a conduit to become a potent power cell for inner change?

In this Infinity Wave practice, you will learn how to tap into the Earth's energy to strengthen you for what needs to be done, whether it is kicking an old habit or getting through your workday. One woman told me that after two years of searching for ways to overcome her alcohol addiction, she credited this practice alone with helping her to finally stop drinking.

You will be receiving Earth energies and transmuting

them through your body, which is a humbling process. This is not something you create; rather, it is something you allow and participate in so that as a walking power cell, you can create positive change wherever you go.

Practice 7: Crystal Columns

This practice addresses our divinity and the balancing of the masculine and feminine within us. It is designed to help you "go direct," and, to me, is the most sacred of all practices.

One of the messages that Yeshua delivered to me was that although He had every intention of including the feminine energy that emanates from Mother Earth in his work, unfortunately it was minimized and left behind by others. He was very clear that it is extremely important that the feminine energetics come alive within each one of us to effect more profound global change.

In a vision, Yeshua and Mary Magdalene showed themselves pouring equally into a crystalline column of light. The message was that the Second Coming prophesized for thousands of years will not be found in the form of a man walking around on this planet like Yeshua did. On the contrary, the Second Coming already IS a balanced masculine/feminine "Christ Consciousness" that is available within each of us.

"What exactly is Christ Consciousness?" I asked. Here is their answer:

"Imagine a beam of light that is made purely of love...

Imagine that beam resides within you and cannot help but radiate in all directions...

Imagine you are a column made of crystal, and you are energized and radiating...

That is Christ Consciousness."

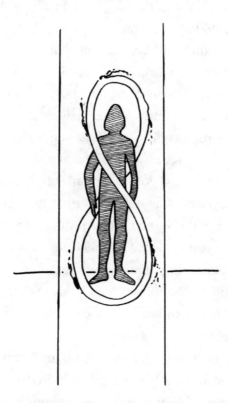

Practice 8: Journey to Your Grace Garden

The more unburdened we are by accumulated aspects of ourselves that weigh us down, the better we can show up in our lives as clear and conscious conduits. To this end, it is sometimes necessary to "clean house" by inviting memories, relationships, and beliefs that are no longer useful to make their exit. At times, this process can invoke sad or uncomfortable past experiences, but this Wave practice does not dwell in the pain of them; it simply acknowledges their presence and offers a loving and compassionate avenue for them to travel out on. People have successfully released deeply held childhood traumas as a result of this meditation.

This is profound and committed work which, from my experience, is 100% worth it. It was in accomplishing my urgent mission to "clean my inner bowl" that cleared the way to receive the Infinity Wave visions that immediately followed. Without having done that scouring, there would not have been room for anything else to come in.

I am gently nudging you to embark on a similar journey with the willingness of an adventurer in pursuit of your own communication with Source. Seek to uncover the brilliance that lies within you—all that is called for in uncovering that gem is some scrubbing! Patience is required because what needs liberating can be stubborn and may take more than one sitting. Yes, it needs to go, but we often have an attachment to it simply because it is familiar.

As you attain more clarity, you gain a better sense of purpose; as you attain a better sense of purpose, you become a more connected conduit, aka the glowing being that you came here to be. The Infinity Wave enables this process to flow smoothly, easily, and relatively painlessly.

I suggest that upon completion of this practice, you take a quiet hour or more to digest and write down what happened. It is very useful to be able to look back later to understand and appreciate what you have just permanently released.

Practice 9: The Infinity Wheel

Do you envision a world of peace? The Infinity Wave can help make it a reality!

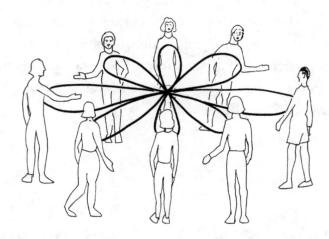

Knowing the powerful connectivity that occurs when you run the Wave with one other person, imagine what would happen if you gathered several people together! Indeed, no other practice I know of instantly brings a group into cohesion like this one.

Imagine eight people standing in a circle, each sending an Infinity Wave from their heart to the heart of the person opposite them. If you were to float overhead, you would look down and see an eight-petaled flower.

The next step is for the edges of the petals to get connected by a gold band that wraps around the circle through everyone's hearts, effectively connecting all hearts and waves into a giant Infinity Wheel.

The rest of the practice enables you to send this wheel off wherever it is most needed.

I know that many of you are interested in doing what you can to heal the strife that occurs on this planet, and even though each one of us can send a Wave anywhere, the impact is much greater when many are gathered in cohesive intention. Use this practice with a group to compound the intention of Love and Compassion to wherever it needs to go. It all starts with you, and it truly does take a village to effect global change. I hope you will share it widely—the more people doing this, the better!

Endnotes

1. I have adapted this description of Pranic breathing from the work of Tom Kenyon and ZaKaiRan. 16 See Kenyon, Tom. The Hathor Material: Messages from an Ascended Civilization. Orb Publications, 2012. OR http://tinyurl.com/bvxr5cy

FIVE
when source
has a plan for you

When it comes to living hand-in-hand with Source, it can often feel like a blind stumble down a breadcrumb trail that might be leading nowhere, until the moment it is revealed that there was a plan all along. I want to share one small example of how saying "yes" to Source's direction showed me that there was a larger significance to all this Waving activity.

I will not go into the entire story here, but in 2012 Jan and I received guidance to appear at Avebury Circle (in the UK) at noon on Lunar Beltane. We were told only that we would deliver a practice of some sort, and though we were not in the habit of traveling across the Atlantic with so little information, we dutifully obeyed. All we knew was that the ancient Celtic tradition of Beltane was determined by the moon cycles, and in 2012 it would fall on May 5 (or 5/5/5, if you add the digits of the year together).

I had come to rely on practices downloading well in advance of due dates, but as the May deadline approached, all remained a mystery. It was a bit unnerving, but there was nothing to do but wait. Then, at seven a.m. on the morning of the 5th, an extremely powerful practice dropped in. Its theme was forgiveness of the masculine by the feminine in order to create a more balanced future. (The Forgiveness practice is available in the Evolve Now recordings.)

The download spoke to the timing since five is the midpoint, the place to pause before moving backward or forward—and we were in a triple five! We were told that the Beltane moment was pivotal for humanity: would we return to the patriarchal practices of the past or bravely step forward into a new, more equal paradigm?

When we had to choose where to do the practice in the sixty-square-mile Avebury complex, we consulted our human guide, the wonderful geomancer and dowser, Glenn Broughton, and my dowsing rods for direction about where to enact the practice. As Glenn listed at least eight potential locations, the rods indicated "No" to each, and I started to get nervous that this had all been a crazy idea. Then he said, "Well, there's a crop circle…" and whoosh, the rods quickly affirmed that we should go there. It had occurred two weeks prior and was the first crop circle of the season.

We entered it precisely at noon and did the Forgiveness pratice, unaware of the circle's design. Only afterward did we look up the aerial photos to see that the crop circle was a twelve-petaled flower within a twelve-petaled flower.

What blew our minds was that we had been working with *that exact design* throughout the previous year in our workshops, often with twelve people in our Waving circle! This could not be a random event, but a synchronous signal to us that we were on the right track, in a dance with something so huge I could not even begin to label or explain it. All I could do was buckle my seatbelt and go for the ride, exclaiming, "Yes!" all the way.

Then, on the morning of my return to the US, I happened to glimpse the image of a purple eight on my Facebook page. Upon closer inspection, I saw this:

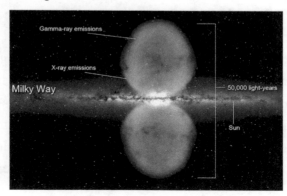

According to space scientist Paul La Violette, in a CNN interview recorded in November of 2010 (coincident with when the Wave arrived), this image was the first-ever clear view of our Galactic Center. The interview has since been scrubbed from the internet for reasons I do not understand, but the photo revealed a giant burst of microwave energy emanating from the Galactic core, ballooning out in all directions and forming the purple "8." This blast, it was explained, was swiftly moving through the galaxy and heating up everything in its path, turning yellow suns into red giants and red giants into brown dwarves.

I had already learned that Russian and Chinese scientists such as Dr. Chiang Kanzchen had shown that microwave energy can not only speed up the evolutionary process but also convert and share DNA from one species to another, such as a duck's physical traits being imprinted onto a chicken.[1] Unfortunately, evidence of these experiments is also impossible to find on the internet now, but I saw the photos before photoshop emerged.

Furthermore, ice cores and fossils have revealed that Galactic blasts like this one have occurred at fairly regular intervals throughout time, possibly causing certain leaps of evolution. As I gazed at those purple "8" balloons, I realized that the Infinity Wave was both a metaphoric energetic and a very real "push of evolution" as my first vision had said. *Holy wow.*

Combined with the Avebury experience, these messages encouraged me to step fully into trust that I would be led exactly where I needed to be. That is when I fully embraced that only when the decision is made to stand firmly apart from doubt and fear, can true freedom emerge.

I tell these stories to encourage you to step forward without hesitation into a deeper relationship with Source, knowing that the more you lean into that loving acceptance, the more it will be increasingly obvious to you that it has your back. Always has, always will.

Endnotes

1. See Wilcock, David. The Source Field Investigations. Dutton, 2011. https://avalonlibrary.17 net/ebooks

epilogue

In my introduction, I said I would reveal why I did not get this book out sooner. Truth be told, I did not want to write it *at all*, but Yeshua and Mary told me to do it, and it is impossible to say no to them. Still, I dragged my heels, afraid of what might happen if I released it. As I came to discover, I had ancient memories of unspeakable things being done to me when I had spoken out in the past and I needed to evolve out of that fear this time around. I am beyond happy to be able to release this book to you now.

In conclusion, more than anything, I want to wish you well on your evolutionary journey now that you have a tool to help you internally navigate the continued chaos of the external world. Remembering that we are all in this transitioning phase together may help should you ever feel alone in this pursuit: *we came here together to do this.*

I would also like to mention something that no one ever told me when I was embarking on my spiritual path: the further and deeper you go, the more unpredictable the journey becomes. I tell you this not to discourage you, but to prepare you ahead of time so you are not surprised when it inevitably happens.

When we first awaken to and align with Spirit, there is

a delightful honeymoon phase when synchronicities are abundant, and we operate in a blissful state much of the time. We may even feel like we've got a handle on this spirituality thing, and it is all gravy from here on out—Life is explained!

It is certainly a time to be treasured, but it is not the endgame...

You see, once hooked by Source, you will be tested. And tested and tested. In the testing, the diamond that is you will be honed as your frequency quickens and deepens. As your vibration becomes more refined, those who are close to you may no longer seem to understand you, nor you them. Do not be surprised if friends and even family members create some distance, or if you suddenly desire to move somewhere you never imagined or discover a new career calling.

Once you start the engine of change, all kinds of things begin to move out of stasis. Your intuition will guide you in these transitions—trust it. Some of them will make logical sense, while others could remain a (sometimes painful) mystery, but I assure you that there will be a wisdom to it in the long run. Remember—through it all, you are being lovingly held by Source, even though it may not be apparent to your conscious mind in the moment.

What matters most of all is that *you come to terms with why you are here as a soul and how you can best serve this world with the skills and talents that are uniquely yours.*

In grasping the answer to this question, you will naturally begin to burn more brightly, like the beacons the guides spoke of in their very first transmission.

I hope you take the Infinity Wave with you into each

question, each relationship, and especially into your heart, so that you can continually be showered with the infinite Love and Compassion it holds.

As for me, I will now begin to write the next book, which will be a longer story about all the magical, paranormal experiences I had along the way since the Infinity Wave arrived. Stay tuned!

I send you infinite Love and blessings for your journey!

about the author

Hope Fitzgerald

Since her spiritual awakening at the Findhorn Foundation in 1976, Hope has been a dedicated seeker of truth, healing and wisdom. For decades, she's been opening her channel to higher guidance through Intuitive Dowsing, and her spiritual teaching and coaching with this tool has helped people transform their lives. Then, in 2010, Hope received a series of visions: first, a massive wave on its way to Earth, representing an incoming evolutionary push for the planet, which ultimately morphed into a standing figure "8" made of flowing water. Through dowsing, it was revealed that this moving geometry was a 10th-dimensional energetic tool called the Infinity Wave, sent to us by a benevolent Universe to more quickly and easily transform pain and suffering into joy and freedom during tumultuous times (which are upon us now). Hope then launched the Wave Energy Center for Conscious Evolution, dedicated to applying the Infinity Wave for the spiritual evolution of the individual, the community and the Earth. Hope has led many workshops and appeared on dozens of international internet and radio shows, continuing to fulfill her mission to encourage individual and planetary awakening around the globe.

Among other things, Hope offers her services as a spiritual teacher, a channeler and medium, a dowser, a Death Doula, and a neurofeedback practitioner. In addition, she guides intimate groups to potent areas around the world, including Peru, Easter Island, South Africa, France, England, Ireland, Scotland, Wales and various U.S. locations. During these spiritual adventures, she teaches ways to communicate with the natural world, believing that when the powerhouse of the human heart interacts with a highly charged site, an alchemy occurs that is guaranteed to cause a shift in consciousness.

Connect with Hope

www.spreadinfinitehope.com

info@we-infinity.com

203-981-7719